BECOMING HUMAN

BECOMING HUMAN

The Healing Journey into the Orthodox Church

By
Jeremy McKemy

Published by Orthodox Road
1150 37th Ave. Dr. NE
Hickory, NC 28601

www.orthodoxroad.com

TABLE OF CONTENTS

Acknowledgments...7
Preface 9
Being Human.. 11

    1. Life According to Nature.. 13
    2. Life Contrary to Nature 19
    3. The Cure for Sin & Death 22
    4. Life above Nature..26

The Healing Journey.. 35

    1. The Church: A Spiritual Hospital 37
    2. The Role of the Body 52
    3. The Role of Our Free Will 60
    4. The Role of Effort and Asceticism 66
    5. The Role of Prayer...73
    6. The Role of Humility..82

Made for Love 95

    1. God's Love for Man..97
    2. Man's Love for God.. 101
    3. Man's Love for Neighbor..................................... 107
    4. Becoming Truly Human 115

Appendix A: On God and the Holy Trinity 119
Appendix B: Baptism...135
Appendix C: Why Did Christ Die on the Cross? 151
Appendix D: A Letter to Charismatics 171
Appendix E: Will All Be Saved? 175
Bibliography 202

ACKNOWLEDGMENTS

I would like to thank Drs. Harry Boosalis and David Ford at St. Tikhon's Orthodox Theological Seminary for their wisdom, input, encouragement, and guidance. The vision for this book, as well as most of the material in it, was reviewed and critiqued by them while I was a student at STOTS.

Also, without the love and support of my wife, none of this would have been possible. As my best friend, she aids me in my journey to draw closer to God.

PREFACE

Our humanity is broken and sickly. A quick glance around us, at the news, or an honest glance inward confirms this sad reality. Corporations, politicians, and well-meaning friends offer solutions that frequently leave us feeling empty and unfulfilled. However, the time-tested beliefs and practices of the Orthodox Church offer us hope, healing, and freedom.

Questions that will be answered in these pages include: What does it mean to be human? Why do we fall short? How can we find healing? What does a healed person look like?

When medical professionals begin their academic training, it often starts with the study of a healthy human body. We cannot understand deviations without knowing there is a norm to deviate from. Therefore, the Orthodox response to the anthropological question begins with pre-fallen humanity in the Garden of Eden. And that is where the first section of this book begins.

After the diagnosis and cure are presented, we will see how the Church herself plays a crucial role in the healing of humanity. The Church is a hospital for the soul through her healing doctrine, living Tradition, and vivifying sacraments. The human body - often neglected or even despised in heterodox religions - is shown to be a vessel of the grace of God that aids our sanctification. Love and communion with God are made possible by a will that freely chooses God. Through our effort and asceticism, we prepare the heart to be receptive to Christ's healing presence within us.

Additionally, the path of healing and life is presented in a practical way through the daily discipline of prayer. Such prayer aids in the acquiring of the most elevated virtues of humility and love, which restore in us the image and likeness of God. Only by living in the manner prescribed for us by our Creator can we find the healing and life that every heart yearns for.

Lastly, because this work was revised in late 2021 to be used as a catechetical aid, appendices have been added that address theological issues for potential converts exploring the Orthodox Church.

Section 1

BEING HUMAN

1

Life According to Nature

M ost of us have heard the story of Adam, Eve, and the peaceful Garden of Eden. The idea that man[1] dwelt in a paradisiacal state for some time is not exclusive to either Christianity or Judaism. The Greek poets, too, spoke of a "golden race of mortal men" who lived in peace with the gods and one another.[2] Other creation myths, such as those of some Native Americans, also speak of a brief time in which humanity existed in peace.[3] Across several

---

[1] Throughout this work, "man" or "mankind" is often used in the classical sense to refer to humanity. It has been the practice throughout the world and for millennia to use "man" (or its linguistic equivalent) to refer either (1) to an individual male or (2) to all humanity, male and female. I have chosen to preserve this traditional usage in this work because many sources I quoted were written before the 20th century's drive to be politically correct. Additionally, it is the most gender-neutral and least restrictive way to use the term.

[2] Hesiod, *Works and Days*, 11.

[3] For more information, see *Native North American Spirituality of the Eastern Woodlands*, Elisabeth Tooker and

cultures, we see a common theme that things used to be better but have deteriorated. It was not until the modern era that the myth of progress gave humanity a different narrative – that man is evolving from ruthless savage to enlightened demi-god.[4]

This commonality between Paganism and Christianity acknowledges a universal human experience; the ancient people of many cultures had this memory of a lost paradise deep within them. We, too, long for this paradise, and it shows in a variety of ways - through art, beautifying our surroundings, poetry, music, entertainment, and even utopian political promises. Through these little yearnings for paradise, humanity frequently seeks to incarnate what we instinctively know we lost. St. Theophan the Recluse explains it this way:

> In the sensual part of the soul, there appears a yearning and love for the beautiful...The eye does not want to tear itself away from the flower and the ear does not want to tear itself from the song, only because the one and the other are beautiful. Everyone arranges and decorates his living area in a certain way, because that way is more beautiful to him. We go for a walk and select a place for the single reason that it is beautiful...To contemplate Divine beauty, to partake of it and delight in it, is a

Native American Myths and Legends, Richard Erdoes and Alfonso Ortiz.

[4] For a fuller treatment of the myth of progress, see C.S. Lewis, "The Funeral of a Great Myth," in *Essay Collection and Other Short Pieces*.

requirement of the spirit and is its life – the Paradisal life.[5]

THE CREATION OF MAN

Creating man's body from the dust of the earth, God breathed His Spirit into him before placing him in the Garden of Eden. Mankind's formation was unique. Like the angelic creatures, man had a spirit[6] that could commune with God. He could also reason with it, and it granted him free will. Unlike the angels, man had a body, a commonality he shares with the animals. As a microcosm of all creation, man is a hybrid of the spiritual and physical realms - a meeting point between heaven and earth - offering up this earthly world to God as priest of creation.[7] Regarding man's special place in creation, St. Gregory Palamas wrote:

> Man, this greater world contained in a lesser, [is] the concentration into one whole of all that is, the recapitulation of all things created by God. Therefore, he was produced last of all, just as we also round off what we have to say with a conclusion. For indeed one might say that this

---

[5] Theophan the Recluse, *The Spiritual Life*, ch. 11, 55.

[6] Both the Scriptures and Church Fathers agree that man is material and spiritual. The non-material aspect of man is sometimes divided into *soul* and *spirit*, other times it is simply called the *soul*. The word "spirit" here references the higher part of man's soul that is capable of communing with God.

[7] Cf. Ware, *The Orthodox Way*, 49-50.

whole universe is, in a sense, a treatise written by the hypostatic Word.[8]

MAN IN PARADISE – THE EIGHTH DAY

Man was destined for eternity from the moment he was created. While made on the sixth day of creation with the animals, God breathed an eternal soul into man, setting him apart from the other creatures. On the seventh day, God rested. However, we see in the second chapter of Genesis that after the creation of man, "God planted a garden eastward in Eden" (Gen. 2:8). St. Symeon the New Theologian interprets this sequence of events as an indication that Eden was formed on the eighth day, which is a symbol for eternity. The eighth day is not locked into the seven-day cycle of weeks that has existed since the world began. Rather, it is outside of this cycle, "since it has neither beginning nor end."[9] Such an observation is more than mildly interesting. It reveals that man was destined for eternal paradise, never to be bound by the cycles of time.

Initially, the physical world existed in perfect peace with itself and mankind. There was neither death nor corruption.[10] Even the animals were at peace with one another. We see a prophecy in Isaiah

---

[8] Gregory Palamas, quoted in Krivosheine, 3.

[9] Symeon the New Theologian, *Discourses*, 24-25.

[10] "Corruption" is used here and elsewhere to indicate what we call aging, decay, or the winding down of things toward death and dissolution. It may also indicate a proclivity toward sin.

of the restoration to come that gives us a glimpse into the past:

> The wolf also shall dwell with the lamb,
> The leopard shall lie down with the young goat,
> The calf and the young lion and the fatling together;
> And a little child shall lead them.
> The cow and the bear shall graze;
> Their young ones shall lie down together;
> And the lion shall eat straw like the ox.
> The nursing child shall play by the cobra's hole,
> And the weaned child shall put his hand in the viper's den.
> They shall not hurt nor destroy in all My holy mountain,
> For the earth shall be full of the knowledge of the Lord
> As the waters cover the sea (Is. 11:6-9).

All was peaceful and at rest, as it was created to be. Even the trees in paradise brought Adam and Eve "indescribable pleasure and enjoyment. For their mortal bodies had to be supplied with incorruptible food. So their way of living was untroubled and their life without weariness."[11] Such was the pre-fallen state of humanity – immortal, peaceful, enjoyable, and filled with wonder. This was life *according to nature.*

St. Gregory of Nyssa writes of Adam being in paradise: "There was in him the godlike beauty of the noetic nature commingled with some ineffable

---

[11] Symeon the New Theologian, op. cit., 26.

power."[12] Adam and Eve's enjoyments were bodily as well as spiritual. If our ancestors had remained in this state, they would have been glorified in God as their communion with Him deepened daily. As St. Symeon wrote, "The soul of each would have become brighter, and the physical body of each altered and changed into an immaterial and spiritual one, into something beyond the physical."[13] However, before they could attain to such an elevated state *above nature*, they fell into sin, halting their divine ascent.

---

[12] Gregory of Nyssa, *Catechetical Discourse*, 6.5.
[13] Ibid., 23.

2

Life Contrary to Nature

---◆---

Adam and Eve's state *according to nature* soon ended. To this day, we live with the consequences of that fateful fall in the Garden. Adam and Eve were tempted by the serpent to eat the fruit of the forbidden tree, being promised, "You will be as gods, knowing good and evil" (Gen. 3:5). Thinking their loving Creator was withholding something better from them - divinity itself - they attempted to grasp the lofty prize without God. Instead, by disobeying the one command they had been given, they fell out of their joyous state of grace. The glory that once clothed them in divine brightness fell away, and they realized they were naked.[14] Communion with God was severed, and they experienced spiritual death, for "separation from God is death."[15] Therefore, they hid in shame from God.

As the sun was beginning to set, and darkness creeped across the earth, our Lord walked into the

---

[14] Cf. Ephraim the Syrian, *Hymns on Paradise*, 6.9.
[15] Irenaeus, *Against Heresies*, Book V, 27.2.

Garden, seeking Adam and Eve.[16] He desired their repentance and restoration.[17] However, instead of admitting their error, they evaded all responsibility. Adam blamed both God and Eve by saying "the woman you gave me" (Gen. 3:11), and Eve blamed the serpent. Neither one of them would admit to their sin.

In this third chapter of Genesis, we learn of two types of death: one of body and the other of soul.[18] God forewarned them, "But of the tree of the knowledge of good and evil you shall not eat, for in the day that you eat of it you shall surely die" (Gen. 2:17). Accordingly, they experienced spiritual death that day. While bodily death would come many years later, St. Symeon tells us, "In soul Adam died immediately."[19] Spiritual death is far worse than bodily since it has eternal implications: "the death of the soul is the separation from it of the Holy Spirit."[20] Since God is the source of all life, joy, and goodness, the lack of His presence within us is the source of every sort of inward darkness. This separation from God is the cause of all death and evil in the world. It is a mode of existence *contrary to nature*.[21]

---

[16] The LXX for Gen. 3:8 indicates that God came "in the afternoon" and the MAS states "in the cool of the day," which would imply the beginning or end of the day.

[17] Symeon the New Theologian, *Discourses*, 27. Also, Theophilus of Antioch, *To Autolycus*, Book 2.26.

[18] Symeon the New Theologian, *First Created Man*, 44.

[19] Ibid., 45.

[20] Ibid.

[21] Irenaeus, *Against Heresies*, Book V, 1.1.

God, in His wisdom, then placed the remainder of creation in a state of corruption.[22] Mankind was made to lovingly rule over creation, which would not be possible within the inverse relationship of unfallen creation and fallen man. Unwillingly, creation was brought into subjection; as St. Paul writes, "For the creation was subjected to futility, not willingly, but because of Him who subjected it in hope" (Rom. 8:20).

Creation secretly held within it a *hope* that all things would be restored. The promise of restoration surrounded humanity through threads divinely woven into the tapestry of creation. Every year, nature appears to die in the winter, but that death culminates in the resurrection of spring. Likewise, the burial of seed bodies in the soil that later burst forth into new life reminds us of a bodily resurrection. As an ultimate attestation of God's hope, even the decaying of organisms creates nutrients in the soil, which make new life possible. We are surrounded by lessons within creation that death can be transformed into life. But until the coming of the "expectation of the nations,"[23] a veil remained over humanity's understanding.[24]

---

[22] Symeon the New Theologian, *Discourses*, 28-29; Silouan the Athonite, 122.
[23] Gen. 49:10, LXX.
[24] Cf. 2 Cor. 3:14-16.

3

The Cure for Sin & Death

Trembles of excitement resounded throughout the earth when its Creator dwelt among us. At His birth, the heavens and the earth rejoiced. The end of death and corruption was not yet, but the cure had been revealed. We see hints of creation's love for its Creator throughout our Lord's life. For example, He states that if the people did not praise Him during His triumphal entry into Jerusalem, the rocks would cry out (Luke 19:40); when he was nailed to the Cross, the sun could not bear the sight and hid (Matt. 27:45); when He gave up His spirit, the earth shook and trembled at what we did to God, the rocks splitting in terror (Matt. 27:51). Though many people did not recognize Him, the creation knew its Creator. After all, it had never ceased to be a witness of God to all mankind (cf. Rom. 1:20). St. Athanasius also attests to this:

> For neither did he make creation itself silent, but what is most wonderful, even at his death, or rather at the very trophy over death, I mean the cross, all creation confessed that he who was made

known and suffered in the body was not simply a human being but Son of God and Savior of all. For the sun turned back and the earth shook and the mountains were rent, and all were awed.[25]

THE SECOND ADAM

The first man, Adam, fell into sin, introducing both sin and death into human nature; as the Apostle writes, "Through one man sin entered the world, and death through sin, and thus death spread to all men because all sinned" (Rom. 5:12). While human nature was created "very good" (Gen. 1:31), the Fall introduced into our nature an inclination toward sin. We lost our likeness to God, and His image within us became damaged. In the words of St. Gregory Palamas, "After the sin of our forefathers, we ceased to be in the likeness of God, yet we did not cease to reflect God's image"[26] – even if that image was faint. However, Adam was "a type of Him who was to come" (Rom. 5:14) to restore the image and likeness within man. Thereby the sin of Adam would not have the last word.

The old Adam fell, and all those born through him consequently enter a seemingly inescapable cycle of sin and death. However, the cure for sin and death brought by the Second Adam is even more powerful. No curse can block it from restoring those who choose to accept it. The Apostle writes, "But where

---

[25] Athanasius, *On the Incarnation*, 19.
[26] Gregory Palamas, *Natural Chapters*, P.G. 150, 1148 B, quoted in Krivosheine, 4.

sin abounded, grace abounded much more, so that as sin reigned in death, even so, grace might reign through righteousness to eternal life through Jesus Christ our Lord" (Rom. 5:20-21).

Jesus Christ - the God-Man - stopped the seemingly invincible forces of sin and death that captured every man and woman, strong or weak, young or old. However, there is a great deal of confusion and misinformation today regarding the true identity of our Lord Jesus Christ, so we will briefly review that.[27]

THE GOD-MAN

The Orthodox Church holds fast the most ancient truths about Jesus Christ. He is the Son of God, the second Person of the Holy Trinity. About 2,000 years ago, the Holy Spirit came upon the Virgin Mary, who miraculously conceived the Lord Jesus in her womb while maintaining her virginity. Taking flesh from her,[28] He was both fully God and fully man. This God-Man underwent all the basic difficulties and temptations that humanity endures, though without sin (Heb. 4:15). His life and death brought Him completely into the human experience. Submitting His human soul and body to God, He provided an example for us to follow. He was betrayed by one of

---

[27] A 2020 survey of American adults found that over 50% deny the divinity of Christ: Ligonier Ministries, https://thestateoftheology.com/, accessed 1/23/2021.

[28] He did not merely pass through her "as water through a tube," which some ancient heretics and some modern Protestants claim. See Irenaeus, *Against Heresies*, 3.11.3.

His disciples and by His own Jewish people to the pagan Romans, resulting in His ascension on the Cross, which was a form of execution designed to degrade and humiliate. Our Lord, however, called it His glorification (cf. Jn. 12:23). He willingly took our sin upon Himself on the Cross, crucifying it in His body, so that its power over us might die with Him (cf. 2 Cor. 5:21). He then joined humanity in death, descending into Hades with His soul. Having entered the darkest places of human experience, He led the charge out of hades, rescuing the righteous souls who were imprisoned in this pit of despair. We sing of this deliverance in the Evlogitaria of the Resurrection:

> The company of angels was amazed, beholding Thee, O Savior, numbered among the dead, who hast destroyed the power of death and raised up Adam with Thyself, setting all men free from hell.[29]

His redemptive work saves us from the corruption of the old Adam and brings us into a renewed humanity. God wished to restore His image and likeness in humanity, as we were made in the beginning (Gen. 1:26). By becoming human, He who always was and always will be God unites our humanity to His divinity, elevating it and deifying human nature. We now have the potential to be adopted as children of God, which will do far more than restore humanity to a pre-fallen state.

---

[29] *The Lenten Triodian*, Matins of Holy Saturday, 645.

4

Life above Nature

———⚬———

One of the oldest and most traditional theological doctrines of the Christian faith is called *theosis*, or in English, deification. Since the first centuries, it has had numerous expositors in the Christian East. However, in the Christian West, less was written on the topic, which is why many modern Christians know so little about it. To understand it, we should first turn to Scripture, which is the cornerstone of the Apostolic Tradition.

SCRIPTURAL SUPPORT

There are numerous hints toward this high calling throughout the New Testament, often wrapped in the language of adoption and becoming "joint heirs with Christ" (Rom. 8:17). [30] In St. Paul's letters, we find that the Incarnation of Christ went beyond restoring creation. Rather, it was taken to new heights. As one scholar wrote:

---

[30] On adoption, cf. Rom. 8:15, 23, Gal. 4:5, Eph. 1:5. On being heirs through faith, cf. Rom. 4.

Adam was a type of Christ (Rom. 5: 14), Christ the second Adam (1 Cor. 15: 45), in the sense that what was wrought by each had consequences for the entire human race. Solidarity in Adam is mirrored by solidarity in Christ, death 'in Adam' balanced against life 'in Christ' (1 Cor. 15: 22, 45). Christ inaugurated a new beginning for humankind, a new mode of human existence: 'if anyone is in Christ, he is a new creation' (2 Cor. 5: 17).[31]

Through grace, we are called to be what He is by nature, which is made possible by His taking on our nature.[32] The Apostle John wrote much about the changing of our nature. Near the beginning of his Gospel, he writes, "But as many as received Him, to them He gave the right to become children of God, to those who believe in His name" (Jn. 1:12). We are not called "creatures of God," but rather "children." Those who are children share the same nature as their parents. Because of our adoption by God and transformation through His grace, the Apostle John could write, "We know that when He is revealed, we shall be like Him, for we shall see Him as He is" (1 Jn. 3:2).

The image of God in man will be restored at that time when we are transformed into children of God. By grace, we shall cast off sin, death, and every sort of evil. The Apostle Peter proclaims our ultimate purpose as being "partakers of the divine nature" (2

---

[31] Russell, *Deification in the Greek Patristic Tradition*, 81.

[32] Cf. Lossky, *The Mystical Theology*, 65.

Pet. 1:4). To be "partakers" of God's nature, our human nature must be elevated to divinity by grace. For a lower thing to partake in something greater, either the greater must become lesser or the lesser become greater. In our case, either God becomes less than God so that we can be like Him, or we are elevated to divinity by Him. St. John Chrysostom affirms that we are transformed and lifted by grace:

> For He became Son of man, who was God's own Son, in order that He might make the sons of men to be children of God. For when the high associates with the low, it touches not at all its own honor, while it raises up the other from its excessive lowness; and even thus it was with the Lord. [33]

EARLY CHRISTIAN SUPPORT

During the first three centuries, Christians were subject to fierce persecutions. Christian scriptures and writings were often burned. Yet the early writings that survived give evidence that the Orthodox Christian faith has not changed. Even in these early centuries, we find theological references to our deification in Christ.

One of the first early Christians to write succinctly on the topic of deification was St. Irenaeus, who was connected to the Apostle John through St. Polycarp.[34] Regarding deification, Irenaeus wrote,

---

[33] John Chrysostom, *Homilies on the Gospel of John*, 11.1.
[34] See #2 of the *Fragments from the Lost Writings of Irenaeus* in which Irenaeus recalls, with great fondness, his childhood

> But following the only true and steadfast Teacher, the Word of God, our Lord Jesus Christ, who did, through His transcendent love, become what we are, that He might bring us to be even what He is Himself.[35]

Since our Lord was divine, bringing "us to be even what He is" means making us divine by grace as well.

This theme of deification was found throughout the ancient Christian world. In the Greek East, St. Athanasius of Alexandria (†373) wrote, "For he was incarnate that we might be made god."[36] Among the Aramaic-speaking Syrians, St. Ephraim (†373) wrote, "He gave us divinity, we gave him humanity."[37] In Gaul (modern-day France), St. Hilary of Poitiers (†367) likewise comments quite clearly on man's deification: "The assumption of our nature was no advancement for God, but His willingness to lower Himself is our promotion, for He did not resign His divinity but conferred divinity on man."[38] In the early years of Christian persecution, St. Hippolytus of Rome (†235) explained deification in language that many modern Christians might find surprisingly bold:

---

years spent with Polycarp who would often speak of his time with the Apostles, especially John, with whom he shared a close friendship.

[35] Irenaeus, *Against Heresies*, Book V, Preface.

[36] Athanasius, *On the Incarnation*, 54.

[37] Ephraim the Syrian, *Hymns on Faith*, 5.7, quoted in Russell, op. cit., 322.

[38] Hilary of Poitiers, *On the Trinity*, 9.4.

And you shall be a companion of the Deity, and a co-heir with Christ, no longer enslaved by lusts or passions, and never again wasted by disease. For you have become God... you have been deified and begotten unto immortality. This explains the proverb, 'Know thyself.' That is, discover God within yourself, for He has formed you after His own image. For Christ is the God above all, and He has arranged to wash away sin from human beings, renewing the old man. And God called man His likeness from the beginning, and has shown His love towards you. And provided you obey His solemn injunctions, and become a faithful follower of Him who is good, you shall resemble Him... For the Deity, by condescension, does not diminish any of His divine perfection by making you God unto His glory![39]

As displayed by the above ancient excerpts, the deification of man has been a Christian doctrine since the earliest times. The Orthodox Church has preserved this teaching through the centuries.

CHRISTIAN POLYTHEISM?

Some modern Christians are hesitant to accept this doctrine because they fear that our deification will rob God of His sovereignty. After all, if we are to be deified, how is God special? Is this deification a covert Eastern pagan belief akin to Hinduism or modern-day Mormanism? Christians since the earliest centuries have been aware of this challenge.

---

[39] Hippolytus of Rome, *Against All Heresies*, 10.30.

They have demonstrated the distinctness of God from His creation by using a variety of terms. Hints of the distinction can be seen in some of the quotes above, insisting that God's divinity is not diminished by our elevation or adoption. Eventually, the terminology surrounding the distinction between *Creator* and *created* was standardized during the fourteenth-century debates between St. Gregory Palamas and his theological opponents. This essence-energy distinction in God assists us in understanding both biblical visions of God and our own deification.

The *essence* of God, then, refers to that unique, uncreated nature of the Father, Son, and Holy Spirit. The one God in three Persons all have one eternal, mysterious essence that no man can ever look upon or approach. St. Paul writes of this divine essence, calling it *light*, stating Christ God is "dwelling in unapproachable light, whom no man has seen or can see" (1 Tim. 6:16). The account of Moses hiding in the cleft of the rock, unable to look upon God's face, is another example (Ex. 33:18-23). Also, St. John tells us, "No one has seen God at any time. The only begotten Son, who is in the bosom of the Father, He has declared Him" (Jn. 1:18). These passages tell us about the eternal transcendence of God.

Yet, even from the above examples, we know that three disciples witnessed the light of Christ at His Transfiguration on Mt. Tabor (Matt. 17:2), that Moses was said to have spoken with God face-to-face (Ex. 33:11), and that prophets and apostles received heavenly visions of God. So, we learn that while God is transcendent, He is also near:

31

"Am I a God near at hand," says the Lord, "and not a God afar off? Can anyone hide himself in secret places, so I shall not see him?" says the Lord. "Do I not fill heaven and earth?" says the Lord (Jer. 23:23).

God's intimacy with both men and angels comes through His uncreated, divine *energies*. These energies - which include God's love, grace, and glory - are an aspect of the divine nature that is made known to creation. The energies allow humanity to participate in God, to become divine, while also keeping a firm boundary between the Creator's essence and created beings. The blessed paradox of God's nearness and transcendence is best explained through the essence-energies distinction, which allows us to hold to the apostolic doctrine of deification without falling into polytheism.

PARTAKERS OF DIVINE NATURE

For some, it may seem that this doctrine of deification unnecessarily complicates the Christian faith. But because we were made for communion and union with God, we must attain to His likeness.

While many of those who pursue a life in Christ will not experience deification in this present life, many saints did. They attained to the likeness of God and were "partakers of the divine nature" in their earthly life. These men and women continue to inspire us through their examples and miracles. Some saints' relics remain "incorrupt," meaning their flesh does not decay after death. One such saint, John the

Wonderworker of Shanghai and San Francisco, died decades ago, yet his body is still preserved by God's grace and can be seen in California. While not many are perfectly preserved, even partially incorrupt bodies provide us with hope. St. Symeon the New Theologian affirms this partial incorruption happens because, until the Second Coming of Christ and our resurrection, even the saints are in a state somewhere between death and immortality. [40]

Another piece of evidence for our hope and restoration includes saints who shone with a divine light due to the indwelling grace of the Holy Spirit. St. Seraphim of Sarov was one of many.[41] Still more saints tamed wild predators, including bears and lions, receiving their aid or keeping them as pets.[42] Innumerable saints – both ancient and modern – performed miracles and healed people, and they continue to do so even after their death.

While we await the complete restoration of all things, God grants us hope through the examples of the saints that we are on the right track. These men and women embodied Christ, which restored them to proper communion with all creation. A proper relation with God places us in a proper relation with

---

[40] "Such bodies may remain for many years, neither wholly incorrupt nor again quite corrupted, but keeping yet the indications each of corruption and incorruption," Symeon the New Theologian, *Ethical Discourses*, 34.

[41] *Little Russian Philokalia, Vol. 1: St. Seraphim of Sarov*, 100.

[42] Elder Zosimus in *The Life of St. Mary*, and the lives of Saints Gerasim, Paul of Thebes, Seraphim of Sarov, Herman of Alaska, etc.

creation as well. A little bit of Eden is restored, and in the lives of the saints, we see examples of life *according to nature* and *above nature.*

Section 2

THE HEALING JOURNEY

Section Summary

*For the glory of God is a living man; and the life of
man consists in beholding God.*[43]

Sin creates dead men. But God wants us to be fully
alive in Him. It was for that purpose that we were
created. To cultivate a life *above nature*, God provided
us with several tools, including the Church, our
bodies, our free will, asceticism, prayer, and humility.
While the prior section traced our creation, fall, and
redemption, this second section will address the tools
God gave us for the healing of our humanity, making
us fully alive in Christ.

---

[43] Irenaeus of Lyons, *Against Heresies*, 4.20.7

1

The Church: A Spiritual Hospital

O ur Lord become incarnate to free us from the bonds of sin and death through the *instrument* of His healing grace. This *instrument* is the Church, which is the bride of Christ. The Church acts as a hospital for souls sickened by sin. The Church's healing role has been contested in the past by morally rigorous groups like the Montanists and the Novatians. However, through the events of Church history, we repeatedly see the Church insisting upon moral purity while simultaneously offering mercy to those who fall. The Church has always preserved the life-giving middle road between legalism and liberality.

PRESERVING THE TRUTH

One way the Church brings healing to humanity is by preserving the Christian faith in its purity. Odd as it may sound, our doctrines are therapeutic and healing for both body and soul. While there are philosophies and religious systems that teach good, ethical behavior, nothing besides Christianity can raise us from the dead and elevate our human nature to divinity. Christianity is the path to eternal life. Sticking to this path, and making no deviations from it, is therefore a matter of spiritual life and death. For those who mix worldliness with Christianity, the Bible warns that their end is "the blackness of darkness forever" (2 Pet. 2:17).

There are numerous ways to express the truth, but there is only one truth. Those who distort fundamental aspects of the faith, that is heretics, have been present since the first generation of Christians. The Apostle Peter warns of the "untaught and unstable people [who] twist to their own destruction… the Scriptures" (2 Pet. 3:16). Many of the epistles in the New Testament address various heresies such as the Judiazers in St. Paul's epistles and the Docetists in St. John's epistles. In the Parable of the Wheat and Tares (Matt. 13:24-30), our Lord gives a warning: there will be those who arise among us who appear to be Christians outwardly but inwardly are full of bitter poison.[44] The Apostle Paul, too, warned the presbyters[45] before his departure,

> For I know this, that after my departure savage wolves will come in among you, not sparing the flock. Also from among yourselves men will rise up, speaking perverse things, to draw away

---

[44] The tare was a poisonous weed that looked like wheat until around harvest time.

[45] In Acts 20:17, the Greek word often translated "elders" is πρεσβυτέρους (presbyterous) or presbyters, who were priests or bishops.

disciples after themselves. Therefore watch, and remember that for three years I did not cease to warn everyone night and day with tears (Ac. 20:29-31).

Yet Christians were not thrown to the "savage wolves" undefended. Our Lord also promised us the Holy Spirit to assist against the enemies within and without, "When He, the Spirit of truth, has come, He will guide you into all truth" (Jn. 16:13). Invisibly, our Lord guides those in the Church through the Holy Spirit, promising us, "I will never leave you nor forsake you" (Heb. 13:5). Again, He says, "Lo, I am with you always, even to the end of the age" (Matt. 28:20). We have our Lord's promise that He is with the Church now and always.

There has never been a time since our Lord's Ascension that He has been absent. Through the Holy Spirit, He guides the Church's leaders. However, this truth is not easy to accept. Due to centuries of anti-Roman Catholic rhetoric in the West, many people believe that the whole Church gradually fell into spiritual darkness. This theory is called the Great Apostasy, and many Westerners unconsciously embrace it. However, it fails historical scrutiny. The innumerable accounts of the martyrs and saints, as well as the great teachings of the Church Fathers, directly contradict the idea that Christianity, as a whole, fell into darkness until the 16th century Protestant Reformation.

Undoubtedly, there have been heretical and corrupt members of the Church. For about a thousand years in the East, and even longer in the West, there were political and societal advantages to becoming a Church hierarch or clergyman. Some men strove for these positions with hearts full of ambition. Yet they could not hide from the God Who says, "I, the Lord, search the heart, I test the mind, even to give every man according to his ways, according to the fruit of his doings" (Jer. 17:10). Our Lord taught us to be discerning: "Beware of false prophets, who come to you in sheep's clothing, but inwardly they are ravenous wolves. You will know them by their fruits" (Matt. 7:15). By the fruits of their lives and teachings we can discern whether they are of God or not.

Ambitious men who attain status in the Church are eventually made known. Likewise, false prophets who distort the Faith are exposed, for the Church was "built on the foundation of the apostles and prophets, Jesus Christ Himself being the chief cornerstone" (Eph. 2:20). The same Apostle also reminded Timothy, "I write so that you may know how you ought to conduct yourself in the house of God, which is the church of the living God, the pillar and ground of the truth" (1 Tim. 3:15). Neither the Bible nor any teacher is *the pillar and ground of the truth*. It is the Church that we rely upon, since most heresies are based on erroneous interpretations of Scripture that ignore Church Tradition.

Every time a heresy has arisen within the Church, our Lord has raised great teachers to confront it. Like a surgeon cutting away cancer, the saints cut away heretical teaching from the Body of Christ – always with the intention of healing and restoring those who seek the truth. The Lord is the truth (Jn. 14:6), and He has preserved His Church in truth over the centuries. For every infamous heretic, He raises up saints to overcome their darkness with light.

LIVING TRADITION

Most heretics utilized Scripture to defend their erroneous ideas. Such a tendency does not make Scripture untrustworthy. Instead, it reveals that Scripture is rightly understood only within the context of the Church community. Heretics invent something innovative, cutting themselves off from the stream of universally accepted Christian teachings in the Church. This stream of truth is properly called *Tradition*.

What constitutes Tradition in the Orthodox Church is a broad topic. It includes the Old Testament, the Gospels, the teachings of the Apostles delivered in word and epistle (cf. 2 Thess. 2:15), the liturgical practices given by the Apostles and their successors, the consensus of the Church Fathers, and the doctrines of the Church councils.

Embracing this Tradition brings us into unity with the universal Church. It is what St. Paul referenced when he wrote, "Now I plead with you, brethren...that you be perfectly joined together in the same mind and in the same judgment" (1 Cor. 1:10). Acquiring such unity requires humility, for we must submit to the wisdom of those who came before us. St. Vincent of Lerins wrote,

> All possible care must be taken, that we hold that faith which has been believed everywhere, always, by all. For that is truly and in the strictest sense 'catholic,' which, as the name itself and the reason of the thing declare, comprehends all universally.[46]

When Christians embrace unity, "they think, feel, and 'speak' through the catholic soul of the Church, through her catholic heart, and her catholic thought."[47] The word *catholic* means whole, or universal. In embracing catholic unity, we find that our Tradition is not a philosophical mindset but a living organism to which we unite.

Let me provide an example. When a man and a woman come together in love, they "tradition" their life to a new child. This life that they give is the life they received from their parents. It is passed along, it is "traditioned" from one generation to another, from Adam and Eve to every living person today. Life can only be passed on by "traditioning" existing life to new life.

Similarly, the Orthodox Church traditions the life of Christ from one generation to the next. Just as God breathed spirit into Adam to give him life (Gen. 2:7), so our Lord Jesus breathed the Holy Spirit into His Apostles (Jn. 20:22), granting them new life in God. The first Adam received a living spirit from God through breathing, while the Second Adam breathed

---

46 Vincent of Lerins, *The Commonitory*, 2.6.
47 Justin Popovich, *Orthodox Faith and Life in Christ*, 212.

the sanctifying Holy Spirit into His disciples. These disciples, after Pentecost, then taught, worshiped with, and laid hands on the next generation, bequeathing unto them the same life in the Holy Spirit. The apostolic generation passed along their life and faith in Christ to the next generation, which passed the same life to the following generation. That process of traditioning life continues to this day in the Church, and it is part of what we call *apostolic succession*.

When we speak of holy Tradition, this life-giving process is what we mean. When we recall great councils and teachers of the past, it is not like viewing ancient artifacts in a museum. Rather, we recognize the living link of the Holy Spirit that connects us to the Christians of the past. We thereby recognize that their life is our life, for Tradition is participation in a divine Body outside of space and time, unified in eternity through the Holy Spirit. All are alive in Christ Jesus: "For He is not the God of the dead but of the living, for all live to Him" (Lk. 20:38). We the Church are one living Body, traversing all time.

THE TURNING ASIDE OF HERESY

This living stream of Tradition can be likened to the healing river "flowing from under the threshold of the temple toward the east" in Ezekiel 47. This river heals everything it touches, "They will be healed, and everything will live wherever the river goes" (Ez. 47:9, LXX). However, outside of the truth preserved by the Church, outside of the living Tradition, life is not found, "But in its outlets and turns and overflows, they will not be healed" (Ez. 47:11, LXX). These areas outside of the healing river, which the Masoretic text calls "swamps and marshes" represent heretics and those who teach out of pride or for personal gain. The flow of Traditioned life has stopped with them, as swamps and marshes have no fresh water source. Most heretics and false teachers begin with at least some semblance of Tradition. But they pervert it, becoming an "outlet" from the stream of Tradition. The Apostle John writes of these teachers,

> They went out from us, but they were not of us; for if they had been of us, they would have continued with us; but they went out that they might be made manifest, that none of them were of us (1 Jn. 2:19).

But for those who stand firm in the truth, who swim in the life-giving stream of Tradition, there is hope and healing. Heretics, schisms, and scandals will arise as long as there are unhealed humans in the Church. However, if we seek God through the Church, He will strengthen and preserve us through the various difficulties.

THE SACRAMENTS

A major part of the life-traditioning process is the sacramental life of the Church. At His Incarnation, our Lord made His material body become the means of salvation. Death and corruption overcame the physical world, yet matter became God's chosen vessel of grace to regenerate and renew the universe. That is why some Orthodox teachers say, "Matter matters." The following pages provide a summary of the Church sacraments.

BAPTISM & CHRISMATION: Our initial forgiveness of sins and initiation into the life of the Church is through baptism. It unites us to the death and resurrection of our Lord Jesus Christ. As the Apostle wrote, "As many of us as were baptized into Christ Jesus were baptized into His death" (Rom. 6:3). After their fall, Adam and Eve lost their garments of glory and received garments of flesh (Gen. 3:21). Yet at baptism, we are clothed again in glory: "For as many of you as were baptized into Christ have put on Christ" (Gal. 3:27). Following the Lord's command, we baptize in the Name of the Holy Trinity: "Go, therefore, and make disciples of all the nations, baptizing them in the name of the Father and of the Son and of the Holy Spirit" (Matt. 28:19). At chrismation, the newly illumined[48] is "sealed with the gift of the Holy Spirit" on the forehead, eyes, ears, nose, mouth, chest, hands, and feet. [49] The thoughts, senses, and actions of the newly illumined are sanctified so he or she may be guided by the Holy Spirit in all things. For more on this sacrament, see Appendix B.

THE EUCHARIST: Next, the newly illumined, along with the gathered faithful, receives the divine Eucharist, which is the Body and Blood of our Lord Jesus Christ. Our Lord said, "He who eats My flesh and

---

[48] Since the most ancient times, baptized Christians were called "illumined."

[49] From the Orthodox Chrismation Service.

drinks My blood abides in Me, and I in him" (Jn. 6:56). Therefore, the priest at every Divine Liturgy consecrates the gifts on the altar, speaking the words of Christ as recorded by the Apostle Paul,

> "Take, eat; this is My body which is broken for you; do this in remembrance of Me." In the same manner He also took the cup after supper, saying, "This cup is the new covenant in My blood. This do, as often as you drink it, in remembrance of Me" (1 Cor. 11:24-25).

The "remembrance" here mentioned by our Lord is far more than a recollection of what happened at the Last Supper. It is participation. The earliest extra-biblical Christian texts reveal a consistent belief that the Eucharist is participation in the Last Supper through the reception of Christ's Body and Blood.

St. Ignatius of Antioch is one of many early witnesses to this doctrine. He wrote his letters shortly after St. John's Gospel was written, and he probably knew the Apostle John. Ignatius' writings affirm that the first two generations of Christians believed the Eucharist to be the Body and Blood of our Lord Jesus. Passing on the teachings of our Lord's disciples, he wrote of the Eucharist, "Be diligent, therefore, to use one Eucharist, for there is one flesh of our Lord Jesus Christ, and one cup, for union with his blood."[50] Of the heretics who rejected this theology, St. Ignatius also wrote,

---

[50] Ignatius of Antioch, *Letter to the Philadelphians*, 4.1.

> They abstain from the Eucharist and from prayer, because they confess not the Eucharist to be the flesh of our Savior Jesus Christ...Those, therefore, who speak against this gift of God, incur death in the midst of their disputes.[51]

For St. Ignatius and the first centuries of Christians, belief in Christ's bodily presence in the Eucharist was a matter of spiritual life and death. No other position can be held, for the Eucharist "is the medicine of immortality, and the antidote to prevent us from dying, but that causes us to live forever in Jesus Christ."[52]

The early Church Fathers affirm the words of our Lord Himself, "Whoever eats My flesh and drinks My blood has eternal life, and I will raise him up at the last day" (Jn. 6:54). If it is mere bread and wine symbolizing Christ's Body and Blood, the Eucharist cannot impart immortality. Additionally, it would do no harm to receive it unworthily. Instead, St. Paul tells us,

> For he who eats and drinks in an unworthy manner eats and drinks judgment to himself, not discerning the Lord's body. For this reason many are weak and sick among you, and many sleep" (1 Cor. 11:29-30).

---

[51] Ignatius of Antioch, *Letter to the Smyrnaeans*, 7.1. Here, "prayer" is likely referring to church services.
[52] Ignatius of Antioch, *Letter to the Ephesians*, 20.1.

Those who "sleep" are those who died from receiving the Eucharist unworthily. A brief examination of 1st Corinthians shows that "sleep" is St. Paul's preferred euphemism for death.

Some Protestant commentators have dismissed the Eucharist as little more than a Church potluck. But that is unreasonable since both the Scriptures and early Christians believed it bestowed eternal life. An ancient, anonymous presbyter, commenting on the Corinthian passage above, wrote, "The Eucharist... was not in itself a meal, for it is spiritual medicine which purifies the person who receives it in faith and with reverence."[53]

CONFESSION (REPENTANCE): Baptism and the Eucharist cleanse us from our sins. However, due to our spiritual weakness and tendency to repeatedly fall into sin, God has granted us the sacrament often called either Confession or Repentance. Through this sacrament, we expose our inner darkness to light. Those who have participated in accountability groups or who have received counseling know the great benefit that comes from a healthy exposure of our sins to a trusted individual. Revealing our inner darkness strips evil and shame of much of their power over us. Not only ancient Christians, but even modern counselors and psychologists have witnessed this phenomenon. Additionally, the vulnerability of confession teaches us humility and provides a path into Christ's healing grace. *The*

---

[53] Ambrosiaster, *Commentary on 1st Corinthians*, 11:23-25, 174.

Didache, a late first-century Christian document, affirms the practice of confession of sins: "But every Lord's day gather yourselves together, and break bread, and give thanksgiving after having confessed your transgressions, that your sacrifice may be pure."[54]

Confession of sins occurs throughout the New Testament,[55] so we know with certainty that it has always been a normal Christian practice. Those who came to John the Baptist confessed their sins (Matt. 3:6). The Apostle James also emphasized its practice: "Confess your trespasses to one another, and pray for one another, that you may be healed. The effective, fervent prayer of a righteous man avails much" (Jm. 5:16). In this passage, we see that confessing our sins is linked to healing. The priest acts as a witness of our confession to Christ. Afterward, he prays for the one who just confessed, as the Apostle James writes above. We confess our sins to God because we know He loves us and wants to forgive us: "If we confess our sins, He is faithful and just to forgive us our sins and to cleanse us from all unrighteousness" (1 Jn. 1:9).

In confession, sin is treated as a sickness, a disease afflicting our humanity. We are not our sickness; our sin does not form our identity. Rather, we seek healing and freedom from the sicknesses that afflict us.

MARRIAGE & MONASTICISM: These two may seem diametrically opposed to one another, but they are

---

54 *The Didache*, 14.1.
55 See Matt. 3:6, Mk. 1:5, Act. 19:18, Jm. 5:16, 1 Jn. 1:9.

not. A man and a woman unite in marriage to aid one another on their journey toward deification. Similarly, a monk unites him or herself to a monastic community to struggle toward the angelic life. In both marriage and monasticism, we are edified and tempted, loved and angered, uplifted and irritated. Our salvation is continuously worked out through our spouse or community. One is a path of celibacy toward all, the other is celibacy toward all but one (and even that one individual does not exist simply to gratify our sexual desires).

In both these paths, God works through the spouse or monastic community to bring us into closer communion with Him. When we are alone, it is quite easy to think highly of our spiritual accomplishments and progress. When we are with others, however, we become more painfully aware of our numerous shortcomings. Likewise, when we are alone, it is easier to fall into despair, but a good companion can help lift us from internal darkness.

OTHER SACRAMENTS: There are other sacraments as well, including unction and ordination. Unction is the anointing given especially to those in sickness, though it can be given at any time. Ordination is done only by a bishop, and it elevates a Christian to a particular office in the life of the Church for the edification of the Body. Neither of these sacraments are discussed in detail because our focus here is on those sacraments a convert will likely encounter soon after becoming an Orthodox Christian.

In the Christian West, the sacraments were traditionally numbered at seven beginning in the 12th century, which was formalized at the Council of Lyon.[56] The Orthodox Church also practices these seven sacraments, though we usually place no limit on the number.[57] God has given us the sacraments as a material method to participate in Him. He infuses matter with His grace, and we commune with Him. In some sense, the entire created world is a sacrament through which we can glorify God and draw closer to Him.

The depth of our communion with God through the sacraments is determined by our readiness to receive Him. The greater we strive toward faith, repentance, humility, and holiness, the more our hearts are opened to Him, and the more impact the reception of the sacraments has on us. Our hearts are like soil in a garden. The better prepared it is, the more likely any seeds planted will grow fruitfully. The sacraments are God's gift to the Church to aid in the healing of our humanity and bring us into the fullness of life.

---

[56] Alfeyev, *Orthodox Christianity, Vol. 5: Sacraments and Other Rites*, 13.
[57] Ibid., 14.

2

The Role of the Body

Because man is a physical creature, God has provided a physical means of salvation. He became incarnate, died a physical death, rose bodily, and established the sacraments to bestow His grace on us through matter. Just as we sin with our body and soul, we also receive the grace of God in body and soul. As mentioned above, many of the saints glowed with the grace of God, experienced incorruption after death, and even continue to stream myrrh from their relics. All these manifestations of God's grace proclaim that God wants to save our bodies, too.

DEFINING BODY, SOUL, AND SPIRIT

Before progressing any further, we should define our terminology to prevent confusion. The body is not difficult to define; however, the invisible part of our humanity - often called soul or spirit - remains largely mysterious. When studying the body, soul, and spirit relationship, we must avoid the temptation to compartmentalize. For "man is not only soul or body but the two together created in the image of God."[58] The body and soul are united to one another, mysteriously intertwined. Met. Hierotheos of Nafpaktos summarizes the teachings of St. Gregory of Nyssa on this subject:

> The soul is not held by the body but holds the body. It is not within the body as in a vessel or bag, but rather the body is within the soul. The soul is throughout the body, 'and there is no part illuminated by it in which it is not wholly present.'[59]

Numerous Church Fathers have provided analytical discussions on the soul, agreeing on all the main points but differing slightly on demarcations. What that means is some Fathers wrote that we have a body and soul, while others said we have a body, soul, and spirit. They all agree with one another. Some simply list the spirit separately, while others include it as part of the soul.[60] In this chapter, I will largely follow the latter model. However, as we examine the different energies or powers of the soul, we should remember the soul is one undivided unity.[61]

---

[58] Gregory Palamas, quoted in Krivosheine, 4.
[59] Hierotheos, *Orthodox Psychotherapy*, 109.
[60] See also Maximus the Confessor, *Third Century on Love*, #32, and John of Damascus, *The Orthodox Faith*, 2.12ff. for a more detailed study.
[61] Larchet, *Theology of the Body*, 14.

The first and "lowest" power of the soul is the *vegetative*, which is common to all living things whether they be plants, animals, or people. It is a life-force, which God implants within the soul that vivifies the creature.[62]

The second energy is the *animal*, which is shared by both humans and animals. It allows for perception of the surrounding world through the senses. This energy can be further divided into two distinct energies: the *incensive* and *appetitive* powers. The former is linked to aggression and the latter to our various emotions and desires. This part of the soul is also responsible for a lower form of imagination associated with the memories of things perceived by the senses.[63] This energy of the soul,

> by virtue of having the closest contact with the body, has become intertwined with it, therefore all the needs of the body are to be considered as its needs, too. That is why we say: 'I want to eat, drink, sleep [etc.]... Having assimilated to itself all the body's needs, the soul considers the satisfaction of these needs to be its business.[64]

The third part or energy of the soul is *spirit*. This highest faculty of the soul sets us apart from the animals. Some Church Fathers would draw the line of demarcation differently, stating we are body, soul

---

[62] Ibid., 15.
[63] Ibid.
[64] Theophan the Recluse, *The Spiritual Life*, 32.

(vegetative and animal), and spirit. Regardless, we are saying the same thing.

The *spirit* is the image of God in man, and it allows man to commune with God. Free will, the ability to contemplate, creative imagination, self-control, and the perception of higher spiritual (noetic) realities are all associated with this energy of the soul.[65] The highest aspect of the *spirit* in Greek is called *nous*. It is often translated into English as "intellect" or "mind." It is the spiritual eye of the soul.

Human beings are a seamless composition of a material, physical body with a non-physical soul. The soul gives life, is rational, can experience emotions and desires, and is capable of communing with God. Keep these definitions in mind as you read through this work and through the Church Fathers.

RESPECTING THE BODY

In Athens, when the Apostle Paul spoke in the Areopagus, he held the great multitude in rapt attention (Acts 17). They were fascinated to learn about this God Who dwelt among men to save them. They were hanging on Paul's every word until he reached the part about the resurrection. Then the majority refused to listen any longer. In ancient Greco-Roman culture, the physical world was viewed as being inferior, perhaps even evil – created by malicious, lower demigods. Most ancient people believed these bodily cages entrapped men's souls. A

---

[65] Larchet, op. cit., 15-16.

God who resurrects the body must be evil since the body is associated with suffering and corruption.

Such a dualistic tendency is still present today. Our culture splits human nature into a superior spirit (the real person) and an inferior or despised body in which the human spirit is trapped. In this system, the soul and body are treated as separate entities, almost like a man inside his automobile. In that example, the vehicle is controlled by the man and it carries him places, but it is alien to his nature. This ideology becomes apparent through religions that seek to free the worshiper from the body, moral systems that treat the body as a vessel for seeking pleasure, and among those who wish to mutilate or surgically alter the body to force it to align with what the mind either wants or believes about the body.

Modern Christians have not been unscathed by these erroneous philosophies that lead to a denigration of the body. In part, it comes from believing that the desires of the body stand between us and God. Other times it is due to bodily infirmity, which inflicts pain or discomfort upon the Christian. Regardless of the reasons, many Christians yearn to be free from their body, and consequently, they have disregarded the body's role in worship and sanctification.

While Orthodox Christians certainly yearn for the eternal age to come, we do so because of our hope in the restoration of all things (cf. Acts 3:21). We anticipate our freedom from corruption – not freedom from our bodies. The body, along with all of creation, was called "very good" by God (Gen. 1:31).

As mentioned above, the saints experienced deification in both soul and body. The body is not a hindrance but an assistant to the soul in prayer and worship. While it has its limits (it must eat, sleep, and rest), our greatest spiritual challenges are often immaterial. Oftentimes, the body interferes in prayer and worship less than the mind, which constantly wanders, daydreams, and recollects both neutral and sinful things during prayer. While our back and feet may hurt as we stand in prayer, it is the mind that constantly chases every random thought that goes through it. Therefore, our bodies are not our enemies.

ENGAGING THE BODY

Orthodox worship engages the body and all five senses in worship of God. With our eyes, we behold the icons all around us, which show us scenes from the Gospel and men and women who have been sanctified in Christ. The beautiful vestments and building adornments recall the heavenly worship after which our liturgical worship is modeled. Our ears hear the melodious chanting and singing of prayers and hymns. The incense wafts through the church, reminding us that our prayers are a sweet-smelling sacrifice to God (cf. Mal. 1:11). At times, the presence of a miraculous myrrh-streaming relic or icon fills the room with the otherworldly fragrance of Paradise. With our hands and lips, we touch the icons as we whisper prayers for our salvation. At the reception of the Eucharist, we "taste and see that the Lord is good" (Ps. 33:8).

Besides using our five senses, we stand during prayer and worship, indicating an active engagement in the Liturgy rather than passive observation. At times, we make prostrations, humbling our entire being through the body's actions. Like the publican in our Lord's parable, we kneel before God, begging for His mercy (Lk. 18). In this way, the body plays a significant role in our repentance and turning to God. The Church Fathers teach that it is the body that makes repentance possible, "For it is owing to the weakness of his body that man comes to have repentance."[66] However, "after death there is for men no repentance."[67] Without the body, you cannot "confess with your mouth the Lord Jesus...[to] be saved" (Rom. 10:9) nor "work out your own salvation with fear and trembling" (Phil. 2:12). Therefore, the body is necessary for repentance and salvation.

We were created with a unity of body and soul to experience God in a way that is exclusive to humanity. Life would not be the same without our bodies. Through our bodily senses, we engage in worshiping, eating, resting, embracing another person, being awestruck at a beautiful sunset, and enjoying the complexity of an orchestra's music. The bodiless angels cannot experience life in the ways we can. Therefore, the life and communion that we have with God through our body and soul is a unique blessing to humans.

---

[66] John of Damascus, *The Orthodox Faith*, 2.3.
[67] Ibid., 2.4.

God wants to heal us in body and soul so that, completely alive, we can know Him to the fullest. What awaits us in the Kingdom of Heaven is unfathomable, for "Eye has not seen, nor ear heard, nor have entered into the heart of man the things which God has prepared for those who love Him" (1 Cor. 2:9). This future life is beyond the knowledge of men and angels. We will know God both spiritually and bodily. Even now, those who devote their lives to repentance and prayer experience a foretaste of heavenly things, as St. Gregory Palamas explains:

> If then the body is to share with the soul in those good things no tongue can name, there can be no doubt that it will share in them now according to its possibilities [that is, its repentance and receptivity] ... and it will experience the Divine once the passions of the soul in accord with the body, have been changed and sanctified though not deadened.[68]

---

[68] Gregory Palamas, *Hagioriticus Tomus*, P.G. 150, 1233 C, translated in Krivosheine, 5.

3

The Role of Our Free Will

———❖———

G od created us to become fully alive by communing with Him. However, He will not commune with us forcefully, for He is love and there is no coercion in love. Instead, through our free will, we cooperate with God to reach our created potentiality. Regarding our free will, St. Justin Popovich wrote,

> Man, for his part, brings the desire, but God gives the grace, and it is from this mutual activity, or synergy, that Christian personality is born... Everything in Christianity is by grace and free will, for all is the common work of God and man.[69]

The synergy of man's willingness meeting God's grace accomplishes our salvation. For that reason, St. Paul wrote, "Work out your own salvation with fear and trembling; for it is God who works in you both to will and to do for His good pleasure" (Phil. 2:12). That

---

[69] Justin Popovich, *Orthodox Faith and Life in Christ*, 133.

is, God works within us to orient us toward Him, but there is still effort that we must make.

Of course, God could have created us without free will, but that would have meant that all our virtuous activity would have been automatic and without any actual love on our part. Free will is necessary for the existence of both love and participation in another being. For example, a man who wishes to find a wife would have a poor substitute in a robot programmed to respond to verbal cues. It could say, "I love you," yet its words would be a mockery of true love. While the risk for rejection and pain is significantly higher in a real woman, she can offer the man authentic love because she willingly does so.[70] Similarly, God gave us free will so that we can utilize our freedom and choose whether we will respond to His love or not.

Due to our sinfulness, our will is fallen and inclined toward evil, which is expressed in various forms of pride, greed, and selfishness. Even from our youth, this is the case, as the Scripture attests: "The imagination of man's heart is evil from his youth" (Gen. 8:21). We quickly learn to justify our behavior

---

[70] This example is not arbitrary. Human-sized robots with artificial intelligence are currently being manufactured as partners for men. These robots have faces that move, eyes that blink, and female anatomy. The AI makes them capable of voice recognition and basic conversation. Similarly, pornography can act as an artificial "lover" for men, and in some countries such as Japan, dating among young people has significantly decreased due to the effects of pornography on the mind and heart.

while condemning the faults of our neighbors. Sin stealthily darkens our hearts and minds, making it harder to choose what is right.

Ancestral sin is the term commonly used to describe the inclination toward evil of our free will. Just as a baby can inherit birth defects from its mother's substance abuse, so we too also inherit a broken humanity from our parents. While the Orthodox generally reject the concept of *original sin* (i.e., that every conceived human being is guilty of Adam's sin), we readily admit that we inherit the brokenness and death that come from Adam's sin.

HEALING THE WILL

Yet, God did not leave this fallen human will without the potential to be healed. When God became man, He did not merely inhabit a human body, but He took on our entire human nature. There is a famous quote from St. Gregory the Theologian in which he writes, "That which He has not assumed He has not healed; but that which is united to His Godhead is also saved."[71] In other words, our Lord Jesus Christ "assumed" (took on) our entire human nature, becoming like us in every way except for sin (Heb. 4:15, cf. 1 Pet. 2:22). Our Lord's humanity was complete. He was not a superman who was incapable of understanding the plight of mere mortals. He experienced hunger, thirst, sleepiness, and every blameless passion as well as every ordinary

---

[71] Gregory Nazianzus, "Epistle 101: To Cledonius the Priest Against Apollinarius."

temptation. He assumed all these things so that He might heal us wholly.

Obedience to Christ's commandments is part of our healing process. Our Lord gave these commands to us through the Scriptures and the Church. In our fallen state, we have often become blind to what is right. Most of the time, we do not desire evil for evil's sake. But our self-centered misuse of the good things God has given us is the cause of evil. Therefore, the Gospel commandments are necessary to teach us right from wrong, and to keep us on the path of life.

Following the commandments of God often requires us to set aside our desires, which breaks our will. Having our will broken, saying with our Lord, "Not my will, but thine, be done," (Lk. 22:42, KJV), begins the healing process. This gives us the means to break out of our self-serving prison in which we are slaves to our fleshly desires and ego. Christ desires to set us free so that we might turn away from sin and overcome it. As we are purified by following the Christian commandments, God's ways become more natural to us. This process leads to an acquiring of God's grace as well as inner peace. His will becomes our will, and the Holy Spirit abides in us.

FREEDOM TO LOVE

Of perfect freedom in Christ, St. Silouan the Athonite writes,

> I learned that freedom is with God and is given of God to humble hearts who have repented and sacrificed their wills before Him. To those who

repent, the Lord gives His peace and the freedom to love Him. And there is nothing better in the world than to love God and one's fellow-man. In this does the soul find rest and joy.[72]

The "freedom to love" comes only through emancipating our fallen will from its slavery to the passions. When we follow our will instead of God's will, we are filled with pride. Such pride swells inside the heart and allows little room for the love of God and others. However, when we crucify our will by living as God commands and accepting whatever hardships He allows, our inner capacity for God is increased. St. Silouan also provides us with a way we can test if we are living according to God's will. He writes,

> How are you to know if you are living according to the will of God? Here is a sign: if you are distressed over anything, it means that you have not fully surrendered to God's will, although it may seem to you that you are living according to His will.

> He who lives according to God's will has no material cares. If he has need of something, he offers himself and the thing to God; and if he does not receive it, he remains as unworried as if he had got what he wanted...and in this way is peace preserved in soul and body.[73]

---

[72] Silouan the Athonite, 341.
[73] Silouan the Athonite, 335.

We must be patient for the healing of our will to take place, for this process "happens by degrees, for grace enters into the soul 'little by little,' being given before all else to the humble."[74] A humble soul trusts itself to God's care. While such a soul will still make plans and continue to complete daily responsibilities, it does so with an acceptance of whatever may occur throughout the day.

---

[74] Justin Popovich, op. cit., 134.

4

The Role of Effort and Asceticism

⸺⸻⸺

The body and soul, with their constant desires and demands, must be held in check so that we are free to pursue life in God. Their healing realigns their focus and energy towards God. But the process requires both God's grace and our effort.

PREPARING THE HEART

At various times in Scripture, we see God's people prepare themselves before meeting God. Before approaching Mt. Sinai, for example, Moses and the Hebrew people purified themselves through washing and abstinence from marital relations (Ex. 19:14-15). The Lord commands us, "Sanctify yourselves therefore, and be ye holy: for I am the Lord your God" (Lev. 20:7, KJV). Our role in spiritual purification appears in the New Testament as well. The Apostle John wrote, "And everyone who has this hope in [Christ] purifies himself, just as He is pure" (1 Jn. 3:3). The Apostle Paul, writing of the glorious promises of God, concluded, "Therefore, having these promises, beloved, let us cleanse ourselves from all filthiness of the flesh and spirit, perfecting holiness in the fear of God" (2 Cor. 7:1). Lastly, the Apostle James wrote, "Draw near to God and He will draw near to you. Cleanse your hands, you sinners; and purify your hearts, you double-minded" (Jm. 4:8). While God's grace plays the leading role in our purification, there is still effort required on our part.

Our Lord illustrates this lesson with the Parable of the Sower (Matt. 13:1-9, 18-23) in which seed is cast upon diverse types of ground. Each type of ground is a metaphor for the receptivity of a soul toward God's word. Commenting on this parable, St. Gregory Palamas teaches,

> 'A sower went out to sow his seed...' But the Lord did not say that He went out to plow the human fields, or to break up the ground two or three times, dig up the roots of the weeds and smooth out the clods of earth, that is to say, to prepare our hearts for cultivation, but that He went out immediately to sow. Why? Because this preliminary work on our souls prior to sowing ought to be done by us. That is why the Forerunner...says 'Prepare ye the way of the Lord, make his paths straight' (Matt. 3:3), and 'Repent ye: for the kingdom of heaven is at hand' (Matt. 3:2).[75]

This working together of God and man is called *synergy*. God calls and we answer; He reaches out but we must grasp His hand. Our effort is what some of

---

[75] Gregory Palamas, *The Homilies,* 47.13.

the Church Fathers meant by stating, "We must, then, do ourselves violence," and "Give blood and receive spirit."[76]

In my Charismatic Protestant years, I experienced much frustration while wrestling with sin. Many teachers in that movement speak of freedom coming from either an instantaneous miracle or simply realizing the need to "name and claim" the victory God has already given all His children. When I converted to Orthodoxy, I found great freedom in being able to confess my complete failure. I no longer had to pretend I already had victory. Orthodoxy gave me the tools for the spiritual fight. If a patient is dying of cancer, he needs medical treatment, not a pep talk. I was dying inside, and no amount of "naming and claiming" could heal me. However, the ascetical wisdom of the Church provided a healing balm. This process of cleansing myself was a crucial missing step in my earlier life.

MAKING THE CONNECTION

Some people are dismayed when faith, church attendance, or the sacraments do not automatically resolve their problems. The sacraments are, of course, grace-filled, but they impart grace upon us only to the extent that we have prepared ourselves to receive God. About this receptivity, St. Cyril of Jerusalem wrote,

---

[76] Dorotheos, *Discourses and Sayings*, 163.

Show in ascetic exercise that your heart is steadfast. Cleanse your vessel, that you may receive grace more abundantly. For though remission of sins is given equally to all, the communion of the Holy Spirit is bestowed in proportion to each man's faith. If you have labored little, you receive little; but if you have labored much, the reward is great. You are running for yourself, see to your own interest.[77]

When connecting two electrical wires, they must be clean. If either wire is corroded or covered in insulating electrical tape, the connection will be weak or nonexistent. Spiritually, it is the same with us. When we feel distant from God, it is often because of spiritual "corrosion" or the "insulating" cares of this world.[78] The discipline of asceticism, however, cleanses our hearts and opens our receptivity to God.

Therefore, asceticism is a tool. It is a means and not the end. The purpose of it is to bring order and discipline to our body and soul so that we can draw closer to God. The Church offers us four fasting seasons that roughly correspond with the four

---

[77] Cyril of Jerusalem, *Catechetical Lectures*, 1.5.

[78] It is worth mentioning that not everyone will see the same spiritual progress in this life. Those, for example, who experience abuse or trauma will have to frequently battle a warped perception of God and the world. They will often carry learned habits of shame in body and soul. Much spiritual progress can still be made, but it may not be as outwardly visible as someone who came from a healthy, loving family. I provide this digression not to enable excuses, but to encourage those who feel they have a steep uphill climb.

seasons of the year. Additionally, we have fast days nearly every Wednesday and Friday to keep us in the rhythm and habit of fasting. When exercising the body, consistency is key. With asceticism, it is no different. Through weekly and seasonal fasting, we are given frequent reminders to practice our asceticism consistently. Our spiritual father[79] can help us develop a "fitness plan" that challenges us to grow without pushing us beyond our strength.

DIVINE ORDER

The discipline that comes from the ascetical life is like medicine for our entire being. When our body and soul are properly ordered, they harmoniously move us toward salvation. When asceticism is practiced in love and humility, it purifies us, making room for Christ to abide in us. The purpose of asceticism is never to kill or harm the body. Instead, to quote St. Theophan, it is "the liberation of passion, the redirection of desire, the transformation of power, and the transfiguration of choice."[80]

Freedom is not following whatever impulses and desires move us. Instead, true freedom refrains from sin. Self-control is much more challenging to achieve than obedience to passionate desire. If sin were freedom, then we could stop whenever we want. Yet

---

[79] A spiritual father is usually the priest of the church that an Orthodox Christian attends. He oversees the spiritual upbringing of his spiritual children, and helps them to develop an educational, ascetical, and spiritual path that will aid in their salvation.

[80] Theophan the Recluse, *The Spiritual Life*, 13.

sinful desires control our behavior and thinking, and we realize we are not free. Asceticism, combined with grace, sets us free by restoring a proper hierarchy within us.

St. Theophan the Recluse lists three types of needs within mankind: spiritual, intellectual, and carnal. All three are natural to us; however, they are presently in an unnatural, disordered state. He writes,

> Spiritual needs are above all, and when they are satisfied, then even though the others are not satisfied, peace exists; but when the spiritual needs are not satisfied, then, even though all other needs are richly satisfied, there is no [inner] peace. That is why the satisfaction of them is called *the one thing needful.*[81]

A lack of spiritual satisfaction inevitably leads us to a lack of inner peace. To compensate, we seek fulfillment in bodily pleasures and intellectual gratification, which only hides the problem. Our lives become a restless pursuit of fleeting pleasures. Food, worldly gain, shopping, sex, music, popularity, and sundry amusements are used to silence our inner turmoil.

Orfield Laboratories in Minneapolis, Minnesota, provides us with a concrete example of what happens when our inner condition cannot be ignored through distraction. The lab created what is known as the quietest room in the world. Most people cannot

---

[81] Ibid., ch. 18, 81-83.

tolerate its absolute quiet for long; the record duration is forty-five minutes. The silence is so intense, people in the room can hear blood running through their veins.[82] True silence is unbearable because our spirit relentlessly troubles us until we are in complete communion with God. The spirit's needs are often ignored, but it will not allow lasting happiness until we turn to the only One who can grant us rest. When we commune with God, the spirit's needs are met, and we establish paradise within us. God created us for communion with Him, and only He can gratify the deepest longing within us.

Here, effort and asceticism come to our aid. We have conflicting desires within us. The desires for both carnal and intellectual fulfillment are innocent and natural. However, their fulfillment must place our spirit's needs at the top of the hierarchy. Fasting disciplines both our body and mind through abstinence from both food and unnecessary distractions. Through fasting, we intensify our spiritual struggle, which aids in our healing. When we practice subjecting the body and mind to the spirit, then we experience the freedom to draw closer to God. To the extent that we draw closer to God, we begin to restore the lost paradise within us, finding life and healing in God.

---

[82] Naha, Namrata, "Orfield Laboratories: The World's Quietest Place."

5

The Role of Prayer

Prayer is the foundation of the spiritual life, for it is communion with God. Since our goal is heaven and eternal communion with God, it befits us to learn how to use this instrument of spiritual healing that fills us with the life of God. While there are several types of prayer, the focus here is on hesychasm. *Hesychia* is a Greek word that means stillness, silence, or peace. The hesychasts were those who dedicated their lives to stillness and constant communion with God. Hardly any of us will become true hesychasts, but it is a goal that is so exceedingly profitable, that even if we fall quite short of it, we will still receive benefit from our efforts.

THE FRAGMENTED MIND

Perpetual noise and distractions fragment our minds and our ability to pay attention. According to a 2018 Nielson survey, adults spend about eleven hours per day consuming media, which is an increase from 9.5 hours per day in 2014.[83] A 2017 survey

---

[83] Brooks, "How Much Screen Time Is Too Much?"

found most smartphone users check their phones 80-110 times per day while spending close to five hours on them.[84] Most phone uses are brief, but that does not make them harmless. Rather, this indicates how scattered our attention is throughout the day. Whenever people have a free moment, they spend it staring at a screen. Such habits make our minds easily distractible, and we have more difficulty giving something or someone our undivided attention.[85] All these traits have likely worsened in our post-pandemic world.

The consequences of our fragmented attention are quite apparent in prayer and worship. We struggle with staying engaged. To keep the ever-wandering mind focused on heavenly things, we should decrease our screen time and train the mind in prayer. For that reason, St. Gregory Palamas believed that – rather than making a list of virtues and trying to keep them – "a stronger means of inward purification, as well as a more vivid expression of our love of God and of our neighbor, is to be found...in prayer...Prayer is higher than the acquisition of particular virtues."[86]

Thoughts fly through our heads almost faster than we can ponder them. While our attention span is worse than that of prior generations, the issue is

---

[84] King University Online, "Cell Phone Addiction."
[85] Wellness Editor, "Screen Time May Be Damaging Attention Spans."
[86] Krivosheine, "The Ascetic and Theological Teaching of St. Gregory Palamas," 6.

perennial. St. Theophan the Recluse wrote in detail about this subject in the nineteenth century:

> Thoughts rise up one after the other, they form into a line, then they intersect each other, race a few steps forward, then go backward, then run sideways, never stopping for anything. This is not reasoning; it is the wandering and scattering of thoughts; therefore, this state is the complete opposite of what our intellectual faculty is supposed to be. That is its illness…[It is] so endemic to everyone that it would be impossible to find a single human being who is capable of continuously conducting the substantial labor of thinking…
>
> People say, 'He is deep in thought.' In reality, he is deep in emptiness, and his intellect is not involved in a substantial discussion of any matter…Observe yourself, and you will see that the greater part of our time is spent on such empty and straying thought.[87]

Being trapped in such a state is spiritually dangerous because it renders us incapable of deep prayer and attentive listening to the Holy Spirit within us. Since communion with God is our ultimate purpose in life, we need progress in this area. Nowadays, rather than the mind idly wandering as St. Theophan described, digital content consumes our attention, molding and forming us for several hours per day. The content we view, even if only for idle

---

[87] Theophan the Recluse, *The Spiritual Life*, ch. 6, 36-37.

amusement, subtly impacts us both spiritually and psychologically. To make matters worse, the social media platforms are designed to be addictive.[88] For that reason, many people are closing their social media accounts and, instead, focusing on the life in front of them. The ceaseless digital "noise" wears down our souls.

DISCOVERING THE KINGDOM WITHIN

Our Lord said, "The kingdom of God is within you" (Lk. 17:21), indicating where we should place our focus – not on distractions outside of us but on God within us. According to St. Macarius the Great, within the heart of every man and woman is both heaven and hell, angels and demons, virtue and vice.[89] But these things are largely hidden from us because we have become spiritually insensitive. The spiritual eye inside of us has become blind. However, through repentance and prayer, we can gradually come to know who we are - the spiritual eye can be healed and opened. Self-knowledge is painful. The darkness we see beneath the mask of the ego reveals a different person from the one we thought we were. But that is part of the healing journey.

In gaining self-knowledge, the wisdom of a spiritual guide is necessary. Books alone are insufficient. The roots of hell go far deeper into our hearts than we think is possible, and our attachments

---

[88] Andersson, Hilary, "Social Media Apps Are Deliberately Addictive to Users."
[89] Macarius the Great, Homily 43.

to pride and worldly desires control us more powerfully than we realize. But the seeds of grace go even deeper. These heavenly seeds of grace are awakened by the light of Christ shining into the heart through prayer, confession, and repentance.

The kingdom of God within us is not discovered through imagining bright, happy scenarios but through the anguish of facing our fears, sins, and failures. When we do so, we begin to realize our need for healing, which in turn, opens a little room in our heart for our Lord Jesus to enter. The more we embrace our nothingness before Christ, the greater our heart expands until it becomes a home for our Lord. He, in turn, brings His friends - the virtues, saints, and angels - into the heart, makes His abode there, and slowly transforms it into a temple and palace. It is a temple because the altar of our heart continually uplifts the sweet fragrance of prayer, and a palace because the King of the cosmos takes up His residence there.

PURSUING HESYCHIA

Recalling the teachings of the hesychastic Fathers, Archbishop Basil Krivosheine wrote, "The hesychast is he who strives to maintain that which is incorporeal (the mind) within the body...The mind's remaining outside the body... [is] the cause of every kind of illusion."[90] The mind outside the body is the mind that wanders; it is distracted and constantly seeks outward stimulation, entertainment, or

---

[90] Krivosheine, op. cit., 8.

amusement. However, prayer unifies the mind and the heart with God, for "the mind which has separated itself from God becomes either bestial or demonical."[91] Innumerable distractions and amusements have fractured our minds, but there is hope.

The fruit that naturally flows from a life of repentance and prayer is hesychia. In that sense, hesychia is the result of a prayerful and ascetical life. We should refrain from treating it as a methodology as some modern authors have done. St. Gregory Palamas explains:

> Hesychia is the standing still of the mind and of the world, forgetfulness of what is below, initiation into secret knowledge of what is above, the putting aside of thoughts for what is better than they. This is the true activity, the ascent to the true contemplation and vision of God... This alone is the sign of the healthy soul, for every other virtue is only a remedy to cure the infirmity of the soul...while contemplation is the fruit of the healthy soul... By it man is deified... ascending through quiet. For by this means...one in a certain sense comes in touch with the blessed and untouchable nature of God. And thus, having purified their hearts through holy quiet, and mingled unutterably with the Light which is above feeling and thought, they see God in themselves as in a mirror.[92]

---

[91] Gregory Palamas, quoted in Krivosheine, 14.
[92] Ibid., 15.

MAKING A START

We all have responsibilities in life that pull our attention away from inward and outward stillness. But there is no need to consider such responsibilities a complete hindrance to prayer. One 14th century hesychast named St. Nicholas Cabasilas worked as a layman in the imperial court while also living in prayer. He wrote:

> And everyone should keep his art or profession. The general should continue to command; the farmer to till the land; the artisan to practice his craft. And I will tell you why. It is not necessary to retire into the desert, to take unpalatable food, to alter one's dress, to compromise one's health, or to do anything unwise, because it is quite possible to remain in one's own home without giving up all one's possessions, and yet to practice continual meditation.[93]

Because our society bombards us with noise by default, "continual meditation" will only come from intentionally managing outward distractions. Phones can be silenced, apps uninstalled, and notifications turned off. A pocket Bible or a prayer rope is an excellent substitute for a glowing screen.

However, when we eventually decrease our external noise, we will discover even greater internal noise: our constant flow of thoughts. Unfortunately, there is no off-switch for these. But there need not be.

---

[93] Nicholas Cabasalis, quoted in Maloney, *Prayer of the Heart*, 56-57.

The purpose of prayer is to orient our heart and mind toward God, not to kill our thoughts. It is the same as asceticism, which orients our body toward worshiping God; it is a movement toward life, not death. Our minds and passions are not slain but redirected and healed.

We should set reasonable expectations for ourselves, beginning with a few minutes for silent prayer. That can be expanded as we grow accustomed to it. The purpose is to focus on one single thought: our Lord Jesus Christ. To aid us in this endeavor, the Church has given us the Jesus Prayer, which is, "Lord Jesus Christ, Son of God, have mercy on me a sinner." Some people shorten the prayer to the holy name of Jesus alone, while others prefer some other abbreviation. Still others will focus on a verse from the Psalms or another passage of Scripture. The mind will wander, so be prepared to frequently reel it back in. Advice on bodily posture varies. However, sitting or standing before an icon of Christ in a quiet room is sufficient.

By the continual practice of inner prayer, many people have developed a profound closeness to Christ, experiencing new life within. No matter where they are or what tasks there are to complete, they continue to orient their hearts to Christ, quietly praying within themselves. Of such a person, St. Silouan wrote, "He may be working or talking but his soul is absorbed in God, because he has given himself over to God's will; wherefore the Lord has him in His care."[94]

6

The Role of Humility

The humble He guides in justice,
And the humble He teaches His way. (Ps. 25:9)

———◦◦◦———

The God of the cosmos - Who is perfect and needs absolutely nothing - chose to wrap Himself in flesh and suffer a humiliating death. This divine condescension is the greatest possible example of humility, for nothing is as high as God and, therefore, nothing can lower itself as much as God did at His Incarnation and death.

Humility is an orientation of the heart that is critical to our becoming like God. It is the simplest of all things, yet the most difficult of the virtues to attain. It is several things: seeing ourselves as the greatest of sinners, repentance of our innumerable faults, dwelling in heavenly joy, the scourge of despondency, complete reliance on God, a heavenly focus, openness to God's grace, and a killing of the cancer of sin within us. Our pride runs deep, closing us off from life in Christ and hindering our healing. The medicine for our pride is humility.

Some of the Church Fathers have said that without humility, no one can be saved.[95] Yet, as St. Leo of Optina wrote, "Where there is humility, salvation is not far away!"[96] The Scripture even speaks of the Lord clothing the humble with the glorious robe of salvation, "For the Lord takes pleasure in His people; He will beautify the humble with salvation" (Ps. 149:4). Humility ushers into the soul the peace and joy that our hearts yearn for: "A humble person lives on earth as if in the Kingdom of Heaven, always happy, peaceful, and satisfied with everything."[97] St. John of the Ladder wrote, "Repentance raises the fallen, mourning knocks at the gate of heaven, and holy humility opens it."[98] However, like prayer, humility takes time to cultivate in the soul. Of this lengthy process, St. Silouan wrote, "The body may soon be made lean by fasting, but it is not easy or possible in a short space of time to subdue the soul so that she is constantly humble."[99]

THE CROWN AND KINGDOM

Humility is the crown of the virtues. When we have humility, we have every other good thing from God. We dwell in a state of perpetual peace and joy, filled with the Holy Spirit. When someone once asked

---

[95] Cf., Silouan the Athonite, p. 298 and *The Ladder of Divine Ascent*, 25.52.
[96] Leo of Optina, *Living Without Hypocrisy*, 181.
[97] Anthony of Optina, *Living Without Hypocrisy*, 173.
[98] John Climacus, *The Ladder of Divine Ascent*, 25.14.
[99] Silouan the Athonite, 302.

St. Paisios the Athonite if a humble person also has all the other virtues, the saint responded,

> Well, of course. The humble person has all the spiritual fragrances: simplicity, meekness, unconditional love, goodness, forbearance, sacrifice, obedience...Since he has spiritual poverty, he also enjoys the fullness of spiritual wealth.[100]

That is why our Lord calls this a blessed state and confers on the humble heaven itself, "Blessed are the poor in spirit, for theirs is the kingdom of heaven" (Matt. 5:3). With these words, our Lord teaches us to uproot pride and lay a firm foundation of humility.[101]

When making bread from scratch, several ingredients are combined and kneaded to form the dough. It is then baked to perfection. Likewise, when forming humility in us, the Lord brings together ingredients such as the flour of prayer and the water of good thoughts. He then vigorously kneads our hearts through obedience and bakes us in the oven of hardships. The process forms a beautiful soul. In the following pages, each one of these parts of the bread-baking metaphor will be explained more fully.

THE INGREDIENT OF PRAYER

Prayer and humility are intricately linked as St. Justin Popovich wrote, "Drawing its strength from prayer, humility goes on growing and growing without end...prayer and humility are always equally

---

[100] Paisios the Athonite, *Passions and Virtues*, 170.
[101] John Chrysostom, *Homilies on Matthew*. 15.3.

balanced."[102] Therefore, prayer leads to humility and humility leads to deeper prayer. Prayer grants us knowledge of ourselves and our inner demons, as written above. Of this process, St. Paisios the Athonite wrote,

> It is the knowledge of ourselves that generates humility. For, the better one knows his own self, the clearer the eyes of the soul see his weaknesses. He will acknowledge both his wretchedness and ingratitude, as well as the great nobility and compassion of God, such that he is overwhelmed by contrition, is greatly humbled, and loves God very much.[103]

As the saint explains, the self-awareness of prayer and humility is twofold. First, it is the painful realization that our depravity runs deep. Such a humbling epiphany causes us to grieve and shed tears of repentance. However, our lowliness before God brings us into the joy of His unfailing love. The soul acknowledges it is dwelling in a self-made hell while simultaneously refusing to tear its eyes away from the sweetness of the Lord's loving-kindness. The truly humble person will then say with St. Paul, "I am the chief of sinners" (cf. 1 Tim. 1:15) while not falling into despair.

The trap of despair is avoided by humility because a humble soul, while painfully aware of its sin and failures, is not focused on itself but rather on

---

[102] Justin Popovich, *Orthodox Faith and Life in Christ*, 131.
[103] Paisios the Athonite, *Passions and Virtues*, 178.

God. Despair is a symptom of pride. This unhealthy sorrow is caused by a bruised ego that does not want to accept how depraved it is. The egoistic soul is gravely disappointed because it imagines itself as being great – or at least not as bad as others. A humble soul, however, will see its shortcomings and be grieved that it has sinned against God and neighbor. It will repeat with the psalmist, "Behold, I was brought forth in iniquity, and in sin my mother conceived me," therefore, "my sin is always before me" (Ps. 51:3,6). In other words, it knows that it has been steeped in sin since its youth and, without the grace of God, is incapable of any good. However, it finds hope in God's grace, love, and mercy, which St. Silouan affirms,

> Without humility, grace is not preserved in the soul, and weariness and despair oppress the soul. But when the soul has learned humility, neither despair nor affliction can approach, because the Spirit of God rejoices her and she is glad.[104]

THE INGREDIENT OF GOOD THOUGHTS

Humility requires us to suspend our judgment and criticism of others. Critical thoughts passing quietly through the heart are evidence of pride, which is a sin common to all. Fortunately, it has a cure: cultivating good thoughts of others. For example, if someone is greatly exceeding the speed limit on the highway, weaving in and out of traffic, I can choose to

---

[104] Silouan the Athonite, 309.

use my imagination in one of two ways. I can either think all kinds of terrible thoughts about that person, how irresponsible, careless, or selfish they are. Or I can use my creativity to come up with excuses. Perhaps a family member is having a medical emergency, or maybe traffic forced him to be late for a job that he desperately needs to keep. Or I can say to myself, "How many times have I also driven poorly or inattentively? God, keep us safe."

Almost daily, we are all faced with the decision to utilize our creative powers to either tear down our brethren or to build them up. We hardly know what is happening in our own hearts, so it is always best we refrain from judging others. Because we cannot know what is in someone's heart, our Lord decried judgmental behavior saying, "Hypocrite! First remove the plank from your own eye, and then you will see clearly to remove the speck from your brother's eye" (Mt. 7:5). A beam or plank of wood is significantly larger than an eye, which implies that our sins are more deeply rooted than we realize. Removing the plank is a life-long struggle. That is why our Lord called it a plank and not a speck.

Those who have been cured of pride are filled with compassion when they see the faults of others. Of such pure ones, St. Paisios taught,

> He who is doing refined spiritual work justifies others, but not himself. And the more he advances spiritually, the more he is freed, and the more he loves God and other people. Then he cannot understand what evil means, for he always has

good thoughts about others, and always thinks purely and sees everything in a spiritual and sanctified light. Such a person benefits even from the falls of others, which he utilizes as a strong brake on himself, in order to attend to himself and to avoid being derailed by the same faults.[105]

THE KNEADING OF OBEDIENCE

Humility requires us to suspend our trust in ourselves by submitting to God and others. We believe that we know best. Yet the Scripture tells us, "Lean not on your own understanding" (Prov. 3:5). In our prideful, individualist culture, this advice is difficult. But even the Apostle Peter writes to us, "Yes, all of you be submissive to one another, and be clothed with humility, for 'God resists the proud, but gives grace to the humble'" (1 Pet. 5:5). Submission to God means following the commandments of the Gospel, and not crafting our own moral rules. It also requires that we follow the biblical interpretation of the Church Fathers, or else we are once again leaning on our own understanding and biases – most of which shape us in imperceivable ways.

Submitting to one another, likewise, is a way to cultivate humility. For youth, that means submission to parents. For all of us, it means obeying our spiritual authorities. The wise Solomon wrote at length affirming the need for guidance: "The one who trusts in himself is a fool, but one who walks in wisdom will be safe" (Prov. 28:26, CSB), and in another place, "The

---

[105] Paisios the Athonite, *Spiritual Struggle*, 32.

way of a fool is right in his own eyes, but he who heeds counsel is wise" (Prov. 12:15). Additionally, God commands us to obey the laws of our nation (assuming those laws do not contradict the Christian Faith) and to honor those in government (1 Pet. 2:13-17). Such commands are difficult in a world that prizes criticism of those in authority.

THE OVEN OF HARDSHIPS

Difficulties are opportunities for growth. When we are misunderstood, criticized, or treated unjustly, we can use these situations as ammunition to shoot bullets at our pride. That is why humility is rarely cultivated while someone is isolated from others. Social interactions, and the difficulties that come with them, provide opportunities for humility to be practiced. St. John of the Ladder wrote, "A horse when alone often imagines that it is galloping, but when it is with others it finds out how slow it is."[106] St. Paisios explains it thus,

> When we pray, 'Lord, give me humility,' God does not take up a measuring cup saying, 'One kilo of humility for you; half a kilo for you.' Instead, He will allow for some indiscreet person to behave badly toward us or He will remove His grace from another who will curse us. This is how we are tested and how we work towards acquiring humility. But often, we do not realize that it is for our benefit that God allows our Brother or Sister

---

[106] John Climacus, op. cit., 25.21.

to act badly toward us, and so we become angry with them.

And although we ask God for humility, we do not accept the opportunities He sends our way to become humble, and we fret and fume. Normally we should be grateful to the one who humiliates us, for he is our great benefactor. Whoever prays for humility from God but does not accept the person God has sent to humble him, does not know what he is asking for.[107]

Prayer for humility is one of the most dangerous prayers. God may answer it, and the answer is rarely pleasant. God sends difficult people into our life to teach us patience, and to teach us how difficult we also can be at times. When giving counsel to someone on how to acquire humility, St. Macarius of Optina wrote, "A humble person is always calm and peaceful, but until we acquire this, many trials are needed. In every situation in which you are agitated, admit your weakness and reproach yourself but not others."[108]

Both difficult people and trying circumstances aid our growth. When life does not go our way, but we say, "Not my will, but thine be done," we experience spiritual advancement. When we accept all that comes to us as God's will, it fills the soul with peace. St. Silouan describes this metaphorically:

---

[107] Paisios the Athonite, *Passions and Virtues*, 184.
[108] Macarius of Optina, *Living without Hypocrisy*, 174.

The soul of the humble man is like the sea. Throw a stone into the sea – for a moment it will ruffle the surface, and then sink to the bottom. Thus do afflictions disappear down in the heart of the humble man because the strength of the Lord is with him.[109]

Similarly, many Christians begin their day with a prayer that was made popular by the Optina Elders:

O Lord, grant that I may meet all that this coming day brings to me with spiritual tranquility. Grant that I may fully surrender myself to thy holy will. At every hour of this day, direct and support me in all things. Whatever news may reach me in the course of the day, teach me to accept it with a calm soul and the firm conviction that all is subject to thy holy will. Guide my thoughts and feeling in all my words and actions. In all unexpected occurrences, let me not forget that all is sent down from thee.[110]

THE LOWEST PATH

Our pride seeks to elevate us while humility seeks the lowest places. St. Silouan wrote, "The humility of Christ dwells in the lowly ones – they are glad to be the least of men."[111] Our Lord was the greatest example of one who seeks the lowly path. As God and Creator of the entire cosmos, He chose to wrap Himself in flesh, to be cared for as an infant, to

---

[109] Silouan the Athonite, 306.
[110] *Orthodox Christian Prayers,* 54.
[111] Silouan the Athonite, 300.

submit to earthly parents, to wash His disciples' feet, to be beaten and spat upon, to be publicly executed in the most humiliating way, and to enter the darkest depths of hades. He could have fought back, He could have called upon twelve legions of angels, or He could have simply spoken a command to send the entire created world back into non-existence. Instead, He showed us the lowly way of humility and asked us to take up our cross and follow Him (Lk. 9:23).

Similarly, in the book *Hinds' Feet on High Places*, water is given a voice to sing. It always rushes toward the lowest places, indicating its humility. The protagonist, Much-Afraid, hears the water singing,

> Come, oh come! let us away--
> Lower, lower every day,
> Oh, what joy it is to race
> Down to find the lowest place.
> This the dearest law we know--
> "It is happy to go low."
> Sweetest urge and sweetest will,
> "Let us go down lower still."
> Hear the summons night and day
> Calling us to come away.
> From the heights we leap and flow
> To the valleys down below.
> Always answering to the call,
> To the lowest place of all.
> Sweetest urge and sweetest pain,
> To go low and rise again.[112]

---

[112] Hurnard, *Hind's Feet on High Places*, 59. Cf. also Lao Tzu, *Tao Te Ching*, 8.

St. Silouan the Athonite, and his disciple St. Sophrony, taught what they called the "inverted pyramid." God was at the top of all creation but willingly descended to the very bottom, taking the weight of every sin, heartache, and pain, upon Himself. There at the bottom of the inverted pyramid, He holds the weight of the world while beckoning us to join Him, "All those who are His must go downwards to be united with Him, the Head of the inverted pyramid, because it is there that the 'fragrance' of the Holy Spirit is found; *there* is the power of divine life."[113]

Even those who have completed great and mighty works in the name of the Lord are told by our Lord to think nothing special of themselves. If we somehow kept all of God's commands perfectly, worked wonders in His name, and even raised the dead, our Lord tells us, "When you have done all those things which you are commanded, say, 'We are unprofitable servants. We have done what was our duty to do'" (Lk. 17:10). Such an attitude protects us from conceit, and thereby guards our closeness to Christ.

Through holy humility, our heart abides in a God-like state, filled with peace, joy, and love. Such an inner orientation brings spiritual healing to us and to those around us, filling all those we meet with divine life in Christ.

---

[113] Zacharou, *The Enlargement of the Heart*, 70

Section 3

MADE FOR LOVE

Section Summary

There is no better way than to live in humility and love.[114]

The epitome of human life is perpetually abiding in the love of God. We were made for communion with the God who is love (cf. 1 Jn. 4:8), and therefore, we were ultimately made for dwelling in love. Our fallen state inhibits the heart from both giving and receiving love as deeply as we were meant to. Section Two describes the process of opening our hearts to God's love through the Church's sacraments, grace, asceticism, and a virtuous life. Everything in the Christian life is - or should be - directed toward drawing closer to God.

Section Three describes God's love for humanity, our love for God, and our love for one another. The focus of this project has been to explore the question: "What does it mean to be human?" In this last section, we come to the climax. Being human means to abide in God and God in us, which is the Kingdom of Heaven. In such a state we find unbounded joy and love. As we commune with God, we learn He is infinite. Therefore, our life in Him is also infinite. For eternity, we will grow from "glory to glory" (2 Cor. 3:18).

---

[114] Silouan the Athonite, 310.

1

God's Love for Man

T he reason God created us was love, and not to fulfill any need on His part. According to St. Gregory of Nyssa, God created humanity "out of an excess of love."[115] The infinite God refused to contain His love. St. Maximus the Confessor also affirms this:

> God, full beyond all fullness, brought creatures into being not because He had need of anything, but so that they might participate in Him in proportion to their capacity and that He Himself might rejoice in His works (cf. Ps. 104:31), through seeing them joyful and ever filled to overflowing with His inexhaustible gifts.[116]

LOVE AND NEED

The Creator and the created dwell in a lopsided relationship. We need God for everything. Every moment that we live, we are borrowing our existence

---

[115] Gregory of Nyssa, *Catechetical Discourse*, 5.3.
[116] Maximus the Confessor, "Third Century on Love," 46, *Philokalia*, Vol. 1.

from God. When we close our hearts to Him, we lose the joy, love, and peace that we were created to abide in. We cannot fully function or be healthy human beings without God. Yet it is not the same on God's part.

A friend once said to me, "God saves us because He needs us. Isn't that a neat thought?" I respectfully disagreed with him. If God needed us, then He saved us to fulfill a need within Himself, which implies motivations other than love. However, the famous Scripture says, "For God so *loved* the world that He gave His only-begotten Son" (Jn. 3:16, emphasis added). God did not *need* the world. With love as His only motivation, He chose to save the creatures who rebelled against Him, blasphemed Him, and cursed Him. We humans frequently come into relationships based on needs or circumstances. Once the need resolves, or the circumstances change, many relationships dissolve because they are not based on perfect love. If God saved us because He needs us, what would happen if we ceased to be needed?

God exists in a Trinity, so He did not create us to fill a need for community. Additionally, Christian theologians since the beginning have taught the immutability and impassibility of God. Those are big words that essentially mean that God undergoes no change. The Scripture bears witness to this as well. Through the Prophet Malachi He said, "For I am the LORD, I do not change" (Mal. 3:6), and the Apostle Paul wrote, "Jesus Christ is the same yesterday and today and forever" (Heb. 13:8). God has no needs. He both created and saved us simply out of an overflow of His love.

GOD'S UNCONQUERABLE LOVE FOR US

The Old Testament prophets beautifully expressed God's love. For example, the Prophet Jeremiah wrote, "Yes, I have loved you with an everlasting love; therefore with lovingkindness I have drawn you" (Jer. 31:3). Likewise, the Prophet Zephaniah wrote:

> The Lord your God in your midst, the Mighty One, will save. He will rejoice over you with gladness, He will quiet you with His love, He will rejoice over you with singing (Zeph. 3:17).

The Lord loves His people and rejoices over them. To enter His joy or remain outside of it is a choice we make with the life we live. All of us sin and fall short of the glory of God (Rom. 3:23), but God desires to save everyone. There are no exceptions (1 Tim. 2:4, 2 Pet. 3:9, Ezek. 18:23). Of the one who turns away from sin and toward God, St. Silouan the Athonite wrote, "The Lord dearly loves the sinner that repents, and tenderly presses him to His breast, and says, 'Where wert thou, My child? Long have I awaited thee.'"[117]

Once we turn to God, no one can pull us out of His hands. We are safe there for as long as we choose to dwell with Him. Our sinful habits and distractions will certainly try to draw us away. But if we remain

---

[117] Silouan the Athonite, 382.

steadfast, repenting when we fall, then nothing will snatch us from His love. The Apostle Paul affirms this:

> Who shall separate us from the love of Christ? Shall tribulation, or distress, or persecution, or famine, or nakedness, or peril, or sword? ... For I am persuaded that neither death nor life, nor angels nor principalities nor powers, nor things present nor things to come, nor height nor depth, nor any other created thing, shall be able to separate us from the love of God which is in Christ Jesus our Lord (Rom. 8:35, 38-39).

The world and our sinful passions deceive us, telling us that we can find joy and life outside of God. However, if we abide in obedience and repentance, we can remain safely in His hands. God's love is constant toward us, though our devotion to Him may waver. When we refuse God's love, we are like the people of our Lord's time who rejected their Messiah. Our Lord lamented over them:

> O Jerusalem, Jerusalem, the one who kills the prophets and stones those who are sent to her! How often I wanted to gather your children together, as a hen gathers her chicks under her wings, but you were not willing! (Matt. 23:37)

His love toward us is steady and unmoving. It's up to us to respond.

2

Man's Love for God

O ur response to God's love is the key to our salvation and the fulfillment of our humanity. God offers love and salvation to all, but not everyone accepts these divine gifts. When we make a feeble attempt to move toward God's outstretched hand, healing love commences. Those who dwell in God's love need not fear anything, for "the Lord preserves all who love Him" (Ps. 145:20).

God not only *has* love but *is* love (cf. 1 Jn. 4:8). However, we fallen humans cannot make such a boast. Yet, there is hope. Both the Scriptures and the Church Fathers clearly show the path of our love for God in a practical way.

HOW WE LOVE GOD IN RETURN

An educated teacher of the Mosaic Law questioned our Lord Jesus Christ. Out of the hundreds of commands found in the Law, what is the most important? Our Lord answered:

> 'You shall love the LORD your God with all your heart, with all your soul, and with all your mind.' This is the first and great commandment. And the

second is like it: 'You shall love your neighbor as yourself.' On these two commandments hang all the Law and the Prophets (Matt. 22:37-40).

For now, our focus will be on the first part of Jesus' response. How do we love God with our *heart, soul,* and *mind*? The primary way we begin is through obedience. Our Lord states that plainly, "He who has My commandments and keeps them, it is he who loves Me. And he who loves Me will be loved by My Father, and I will love him and manifest Myself to him" (Jn. 14:21). A little later, He assures us that this is how we can stay in His love: "If you keep My commandments, you will abide in My love, just as I have kept My Father's commandments and abide in His love" (Jn. 15:10). By living in the ways of God, we open our hearts to His love.

To dwell in love, obedience is required. But that is not because God is a controlling tyrant. Nor are these teachings perpetuated because the Church wishes to control people. Instead, it is because God alone is the source of all that is truly beautiful and loving. All that is outside of God is loneliness and darkness. In our fallen state, we can find it difficult to discern the path of life. Therefore, God plainly lays out the path for us. He says, "This is the way that you become like me. This is the way to become creatures of love and life, peace and joy. All other paths are deceptive delusions."

DWELLING IN LOVE

We can love and obey God with our *heart, soul,* and *mind* by keeping our thoughts on God constantly. St. Silouan the Athonite wrote:

> When a man loves, his desire is to talk of the object of his love; and then habit enters in – if you make a habit of thinking of God, you will always carry God with you in your soul. If you are forever thinking of earthly matters, they will absorb your mind.[118]

Many saints who dwelt in the love of God did not feel as though they loved God. They felt their meager offering of obedience and affection was hardly worth labeling as "love." They displayed their love through obedience to the Scriptures and the teachings of the Church. St. Silouan assures those who desire love but do not feel it:

> But you, brother, be not troubled if you do not sense the love of God within yourself: think on the Lord, how He is gracious, and keep yourself from sin, and the grace of God will instruct you.[119]

The grace of God, mentioned by St. Silouan, instructs us to follow the precepts of God. However, many of us cringe at anything that limits our freedom. St. Theophan the Recluse explained that we "think that rules about the worthwhile life are outwardly

---

[118] Silouan the Athonite, 373.
[119] Ibid., 372.

imposed, and, not springing from man's very nature." We conclude that such rules are therefore not needed by [us]."[120] Yet the commandments are not arbitrary. They reveal what God is like and thereby show us the divine path to being fully human.

The Old Testament king and prophet David was a man after God's own heart (cf. 1 Sam. 13:14). The books of Samuel, Kings, and Chronicles make it clear that David could be honored with this title because he devoted his life to keeping God's commandments. So great was his devotion that most of the Judahite kings were evaluated based on how well they lived up to David's standard.

Those who are filled with God's grace desire nothing more than to be with God and honor Him through obedience. The longest chapter in the Bible, Psalm 119, reveals that love for God's commandments possesses a person who dwells in God's love. Every one of its 176 verses teaches devotion for the statutes of God.

The patristic scholar and teacher Archbishop Basil Krivosheine wrote that communion with God is reached initially by "keeping His commandments." If we want to draw closer to God, we must obey Him. Abp. Basil continues:

> This path (of keeping the commandments) must be followed by all and can be described in short as the love of God and of our neighbor. Off this path there can be no question of any sort of communion

---

120 Theophan the Recluse, *The Spiritual Life*, 30.

with God... The commandments have universal validity and are binding on all men.[121]

THE CALL TO HOLINESS

By their very name, we can see that the commandments are not suggestions. Our Lord did not say, "Do what makes you feel good," but instead He tells us, "Be perfect, just as your Father in heaven is perfect" (Matt. 5:48). His disciple, St. Peter, tells us to be "obedient children...as He who called you is holy, you also be holy in all your conduct" (1 Pet. 1:14-15). The call to holiness is, therefore, the calling of every Christian. It is not imposed on us to control us through arduous expectations. Instead, it reveals the foundation of divine life.

The Apostle James concludes that a lack of holiness, the pursuit of pleasures, and the desire for personal gain are the cause of all division and troubles in our lives and communities. Using strong language, he calls interpersonal conflict *wars:* "Where do wars and fights come from among you? Do they not come from your desires for pleasure that war in your members?" (Jam. 4:1). In other words, not following the commands causes suffering and grief among us because - most often - the commands of God place limits on our pride and selfishness. St. Macarius the Great wrote, "Those who fail to love God will not succeed in loving their neighbor either. They will either be grumpy or proud. I have certainly witnessed both. Love for God protects our neighbor

---

[121] Krivosheine, 6.

from us."[122] When we live for our own desires, it inevitably hurts those around us and drives a wedge between us and the grace of God.

We cannot live selfishly while also expecting heavenly love. When we live for ourselves, it makes us miserable because we become our own gods, and lousy gods we are. The Apostle Paul tells the Philippians to follow his moral example; those who reject the way of Christ are those "whose end is destruction, whose god is their belly, and whose glory is in their shame—who set their mind on earthly things" (Phil. 3:19). However, when we humble ourselves before God, recognizing our incompetence to even rule ourselves as gods, we find His grace carrying us. St. Justin Popovich writes about this grace-filled state:

> The man who strives in love enjoys a foretaste of the harmony of Paradise in himself and in God's world around him, for he has been delivered from the hell of self-centeredness and has entered into the paradise of divine values and perfections.[123]

The virtuous life reflects the divine life. God tells us, "Be holy, for I am holy" (1 Pet. 1:16). God calls us to be like Him. But why? As outlined in the chapter "Life above Nature," He desires our participation in His love and glory. God wants to commune with us as deeply as possible, which requires likeness to Him.

---

[122] Macarius the Great, *The Great Letter.*
[123] Justin Popovich, 130.

3

Man's Love for Neighbor

―――――◦◦◉◦◦―――――

After the love of God, the second greatest command is to "love your neighbor as yourself" (Matt. 22:39). Love for neighbor displays love for God. A major sin of the Pharisees was following God's rules without love. For that reason, the virtuous life must always be joined with a love for our neighbors. It is impossible to love God without love for neighbor, for "He who does not love does not know God, for God is love" (1 Jn. 4:8). St. Maximus tells us, "Just as the thought of fire does not warm the body, so faith without love does not actualize the light of spiritual knowledge in the soul,"[124] which echoes the Apostle James:

> If a brother or sister is naked and destitute of daily food, and one of you says to them, 'Depart in peace, be warmed and filled,' but you do not give them the things which are needed for the body, what

―――――――――――――――

[124] Maximus the Confessor, *First Century on Love*, 31.

does it profit? Thus also faith by itself, if it does not have works, is dead (Jas. 2:15-17).

Of all the works, the most important is love. Therefore, understanding what our Lord meant by love for neighbor is imperative.

AS YOU LOVE YOURSELF

Going back to the words of Christ, we are to love our neighbor as we love ourselves. What does it mean to love oneself? How is society's message about self-love different from our Lord's words?

About self-love, St. Maximus the Confessor wrote:

> Self-love is an impassioned, mindless love for one's body. Its opposite is love and self-control. A man dominated by self-love is dominated by all the passions.[125]

The self-pampering life our society encourages is exactly what St. Maximus was warning against. It is not wrong to feed, clothe, and care for the body. However, when we obsess over it, always pampering and pleasing it, we have become slaves to the body and its passions. Our Lord asked, "Is not life more than food, and the body more than clothes?" (Matt. 6:25) While we need not give up all our possessions as St. Anthony the Great did, we do need to practice discipline with ourselves.

---

[125] Maximus the Confessor, *Third Century on Love*, 8.

When Christ tells us, "Love your neighbor as yourself," He encourages both practical and spiritual behavior. Practically speaking, when we are hungry, we eat; when thirsty, we drink; when cold, we wear a jacket. We should ensure our neighbor is adequately cared for with the necessities of life, just as we care for ourselves. The same applies spiritually. We should care for our neighbor's spiritual needs as we care for our own. That includes showing love, being quick to forgive, and providing spiritual instruction if our neighbor desires that.

LOVE FOR ENEMIES

One of the most revolutionary teachings in the world is the Christian message of love for enemies. No philosopher taught anything like it. The closest was Lao Tzu, who wrote that we should "requite injury with kindness."[126] For most of history, however, it would have been considered madness to treat enemies with love or kindness. Our Lord Jesus taught the perfect love of God, which loves all creatures unconditionally. His words are worth quoting in length:

> You have heard that it was said, 'You shall love your neighbor and hate your enemy.' But I say to you, love your enemies, bless those who curse you, do good to those who hate you, and pray for those who spitefully use you and persecute you, that you may be sons of your Father in heaven; for He makes His sun rise on the evil and on the good, and

---

[126] Lao Tzu, *Tao Te Ching*, 63.

sends rain on the just and on the unjust. For if you love those who love you, what reward have you? Do not even the tax collectors do the same? And if you greet your brethren only, what do you do more than others? Do not even the tax collectors do so? Therefore you shall be perfect, just as your Father in heaven is perfect (Matt. 5:43-48).

God sends rain on the good and evil, He loves all equally, and He calls us to imitate Him in perfect, equal love of all. About this passage, St. Maximus wrote:

Why did He command this? To free you from hatred, irritation, anger and rancor, and to make you worthy of the supreme gift of perfect love. And you cannot attain such love if you do not imitate God and love all men equally. For God loves all men equally and wishes them 'to be saved and to come to the knowledge of the truth.'[127]

Equal love for the righteous and sinners means,

If we detect any trace of hatred in our hearts against any man whatsoever for committing any fault, we are utterly estranged from love for God, since love for God absolutely precludes us from hating any man."[128]

This equal love for all is called "perfect love," and it is divine.

---

[127] Maximus the Confessor, *First Century on Love*, 61.
[128] Ibid., 15.

Such a perfect love does not come easily to us. It requires recognition of our fallen state, repentance, and perseverance. But the lives of the saints reveal to us that perfect love is possible. St. Silouan the Athonite wrote, "The soul cannot know peace unless she prays for her enemies."[129] Such prayers are for the good and salvation of our enemies, not their harm. He continues:

> If you will pray for your enemies, peace will come to you; but when you can love your enemies – know that a great measure of the grace of God dwells in you, though I do not say perfect grace as yet, but sufficient for salvation. Whereas if you revile your enemies, it means there is an evil spirit living in you and bringing evil thoughts into your heart... If you cannot love, then at least do not revile or curse your enemies.[130]

St. Silouan explains that even if people are persecuting the Church - no matter how evil they are - we should love and pity them as God loved and pitied us when we were His enemies (Rom. 5:10). There are no exceptions to God's love, and there should be none to ours. To illustrate this lesson, St. Silouan mentions the example of James and John who offered to call down fire from heaven when the Samaritans rejected Christ.[131] But our Lord replies, "the Son of Man did not come to destroy men's lives

---

[129] Silouan the Athonite, 376.
[130] Ibid., 377.
[131] Ibid., 378-379.

but to save them" (Luke 9:56). We, too, when filled with the love of Christ, will yearn for the salvation of all men. Their rebellion against God will fill us with sorrow:

> The soul sorrows for her enemies and prays for them because they have strayed from the truth and their faces are set towards hell. That is love for our enemies...be gentle with those who err and stray.[132]

AFFIRMING THE IMAGE OF GOD

Both the Bible and the saints call us to be gentle with those who have fallen (cf. Gal. 6:1). Through love for our neighbor, we affirm the image of God in that person. Sin has tarnished the image of God in all of us. But that image is still there. In a world that is becoming increasingly polarized and unloving, we Christians must maintain a spirit of gentle love. There have always been enemies of the Church whose errors must be corrected at times. However, we must always act with the salvation of the other person in mind. When theological battles are about proving ourselves righter than the other person, then we have lost everything spiritually.

There is a story from the Desert Fathers in which a young, zealous monk was traveling with his elder, St. Macarius the Great. The young monk went ahead of his elder on the road. When he came across a pagan priest traveling the opposite direction, the young

---

[132] Ibid., 379.

monk mocked him, crying out, "Where are you going, you devil?" Infuriated, the pagan priest beat the young monk severely, leaving him half-dead on the side of the road. Fleeing the scene, the pagan priest soon met St. Macarius on the road. Discerning the priest's agitation, Macarius cheerfully greeted and consoled him. The pagan priest was so moved by St. Macarius' kindness, that he wanted to become a monk as well. But first, they retrieved the obstinate, young monk and treated his wounds. Afterward, the pagan priest took monastic vows and converted many pagans to Christianity.[133]

This story teaches that love and kindness are always superior to zeal when dealing with our fellow man. St. Paul reminds us, "the goodness of God leads you to repentance" (Rom. 2:4). When recounting the pagan priest's conversion, St. Macarius said, "One evil word makes even the good evil, while one good word makes even the evil good."[134] As Christians, we must resist the temptation to fight with our fellow man who is made in the image of God. Instead, we should see the potential that is in every person as St. Isaac the Syrian explains,

> When you meet your fellow man, constrain yourself to pay him more honor than is his due. Kiss his hands and feet, often take his hands with deep respect, put them over your eyes, and praise him for what he does not even possess. And when he parts from you, say every good thing about him,

---

[133] *The Sayings of the Desert Fathers*, Ward, 137.
[134] Macarius the Great, 379.

and whatever it may be that commands respect. For by these and similar acts, you draw him to good and make him feel ashamed because of the gracious names by which you have called him, and you sow the seeds of virtue in him.

From behavior such as this, to which you accustom yourself, a good pattern is also imprinted in you; and you gain much humility for yourself, and achieve great things without toil. And not only this, but if he has any faults or voluntary imperfections, he will readily accept correction from you when he is honored by you, being ashamed because of the respect which you have shown him and the proof of love he continually sees in you. Let this always be the aim of your conduct: to be courteous and respectful to all.[135]

In his humility, St. Isaac could see the image of God in each person and the virtues that they would attain when aided by loving edification. Practicing this uplifting love will take different forms from what St. Isaac wrote above because our culture is different from his. But the truth remains that we should treat all people like the saints whom God has called them to be, even if we cannot see their sanctity right now. The Apostle Paul also wrote, "Be kindly affectionate to one another with brotherly love, in honor giving preference to one another" (Rom. 12:10).

---

[135] Isaac the Syrian, *The Ascetical Homilies*, 5.

4

Becoming Truly Human

———◆———

St. Maximus the Confessor closes his *Four Centuries on Love* with a final thought:

> Many have said much about love, but you will find love itself only if you seek it among the disciples of Christ. For only they have true Love as love's teacher. 'Though I have the gift of prophecy,' says St. Paul, 'and know all mysteries and all knowledge . . . and have no love, it profits me nothing' (1 Cor. 13:2-3). He who possesses love possesses God Himself, for 'God is love' (1 Jn. 4:8). [136]

Today, we hear much said about love, but to find unconditional, perfect love, we turn to the disciples of Christ. They point us to the only Being Who is love by nature. The world promises us love and personal fulfillment if we follow its ways. But it is like the serpent in the Garden of Eden, whispering lies and half-truths that will lead to death.

---

[136] Maximus the Confessor, *Fourth Century on Love*, 100.

Our society generally recoils at exclusive language, and a person may fairly ask, "What about love among family and friends? That can be found outside of Christianity." Family and friends do indeed love each other, sometimes unconditionally. Such love is possible because we are made in the image of God. However, love among family and friends is merely the beginning of love. Familial and brotherly love point to something much greater beyond themselves.

In the end, like other philosophies and religions that contain elements of truth, these forms of human love have limits. Nothing outside the revelation of God's love through Jesus Christ can heal our humanity, raise us from the dead, and make us truly human. God made us not for mediocrity but for divinity. Through the ascetical and sacramental life of the Church, He desires to transform everyone. This transformation, once fully realized, enables us to become a healing presence to others. Rather than perpetuating the brokenness that surrounds us, God can bring His healing grace to others through us. That is what it means to become truly human.

APPENDICES

APPENDIX A: ON GOD AND THE HOLY TRINITY

——————❖——————

R egarding the Holy Trinity, most Christians affirm the divinity of the Father, the Son, and the Holy Spirit. This theology is the most important doctrine of Christianity, so it is encouraging that we Orthodox find unity in this way with billions of Christians across the world. However, before we dive into the Holy Trinity, we will first address what it is we mean by *God*.

ON WHAT WE MEAN BY "GOD"

Some of the brightest Christian minds have struggled over terminology and debated exactly how belief in God should be expressed. They experienced God, they knew Him, but trying to express that spiritual experience in human language was difficult. To avoid error, negative language is sometimes employed instead of positive. For example, we say God is infinite, incomprehensible, and uncircum-scribed because it is less limiting to say what God is *not* rather than what He *is*. Some Church Fathers referred to God as darkness, not to oppose Scripture (cf. 1 Jn. 1:5) nor to sound esoteric, but to express their wonder in gazing into the infinitely unknowable depth and mystery of God.

A good starting place when talking about God is to acknowledge that "all things are either created or uncreated." [137] Only God is uncreated, so the uncreated is divine by nature. Orthodox Christians believe in one uncreated God who brought creation into existence out of nothing. The one uncreated God has revealed Himself to us in three Persons: Father, Son, and Holy Spirit, which we call the Holy Trinity. All three Persons are uncreated, eternal, equally and fully divine, and of the same nature. More on the Holy Trinity will be discussed later in this chapter.

ANTHROPOMORPHISM

When reading through the Scriptures, many devout Christians will notice that anthropomorphic language - attributing human traits to God - is quite common. All biblical references to God's emotional state, God sitting on a throne, God's right hand, God smelling, tasting, or any other bodily reference must be understood as allegorical. These expressions reveal an underlying truth about God and our relation to Him, but they should not be understood literally. The divine nature is spiritual and therefore does not possess bodily properties that would allow for literally sitting, standing, smelling, tasting, etc.

---

[137] St. John of Damascus, *On the Orthodox Faith*, 1.3, p. 169.

Our Lord said, "God is spirit" (Jn. 4:24) so that we would not assume He is bound by a body or location. However, we do not limit Him to being *merely* spirit.[138] God is spirit but also beyond spirit. Both fleshly creatures (such as humans) and spiritual ones (such as angels) exist within a general location at a particular time in the realm of creation. Yet God exists even beyond the created physical and spiritual realities in a way that cannot be grasped, pierced, or experienced by any created thing.

The wrath of God is another aspect that is frequently misunderstood, especially by some tel-evangelists who blame every disaster on God's anger and judgment upon the world. They speak as if God angrily itches to smite humanity every time we sin. While the Scriptures certainly have anthro-popathisms (attributing to God human emotions), these, like anthropomorphisms, should not be taken literally. God is not passionate, nor does He change. He is not subject to mood swings as emotional and imperfect humans are. Otherwise, looking into the lives of the billions of people on this planet would cause God to be in a perpetual state of flux and

---

[138] In addressing the Samaritan woman at the well (Jn. 4), our Lord was commenting on an ancient debate between Jews and Samaritans regarding the proper place for worshiping God. Most pagans believed that deities actually resided in the temples built for them. Due to their intermixing for generations with the pagans, the Samaritans held certain pagan ideas. Our Lord was teaching her that God is not constrained to a physical temple but can be worshiped everywhere "in spirit and in truth."

121

instability. But God said through the Prophet Malachi, "For I am the LORD, I do not change" (Mal. 3:6). We also read, "Jesus Christ is the same yesterday and today and forever" (Heb. 13:8).

ESSENCE AND ENERGIES

When speaking of a Being who is so far beyond our mode of existence, we inevitably fall into paradoxes. These paradoxes can be frustrating for those who seek tidy, logical explanations. However, the divine Cause of all creation cannot be easily compartmentalized or rationalized. God is both knowable and unknowable; He is far and near; He is within all created things, sustaining their existence, while simultaneously existing outside of all created realms and dimensions. We naturally finite creatures cannot fully grasp that which is by nature infinite and incomprehensible. Something of God will always remain outside of our realm of experience. This unknowable 'something' is called God's *essence* in Orthodox theology (also translated as *substance*). Of this essence, St. John Damascene writes, "It is clear that God exists, but what He is in essence and nature is unknown and beyond all understanding."[139] This essence or substance is unknowable, not only to man

---

[139] St. John of Damascus, *On the Orthodox Faith*, 1.4, p. 170. For more on God's unknowable essence, see St. Gregory of Nazianzus' *Five Theological Orations*, St. Gregory of Nyssa's *Against Eunomius*, St. Basil the Great's *Against Eunomius*, and St. John Chrysostom's *On the Incomprehensible Nature of God*.

but also to angels – it is that which no man can see and live (cf. Ex. 33:20).

Fortunately, we can still know God. Through His uncreated energies, we interact with God Himself. "The grace of the Lord Jesus Christ, and the love of God, and the communion of the Holy Spirit" (2 Cor. 13:14) is an experience with the Holy Trinity in the life of those being saved. In this grace, love, and communion, we enter the mystery of the Holy Trinity; we "participate in the divine nature" (2 Pet. 1:4). Such participation elevates us to a supernatural mode of existence with the end goal of *theosis* (deification) in the life of the Church. In whatever way we experience God, we are experiencing His divine energies. These energies are part of His nature that allow us to commune and unite with God while recognizing the distinction and unbridgeable chasm between created beings and God's essence. St. Gregory Palamas writes, "The divine kingdom, glory, splendor, ineffable light, and divine grace can be seen and shared by the saints, but not God's essence." [140]

GOD AS FATHER

The Scriptures, through divine revelation, show us how to address God who revealed Himself through the prophets, the apostles, and His Son. The Lord Jesus frequently referred to God as both His Father and our Father. For instance, our Lord commanded

---

[140] St. Gregory Palamas, "Second Homily on the Transfiguration," *The Homilies*, p. 281.

us, "Pray in this manner: Our Father who art in heaven..." (Matt. 6:9).

What a joy and privilege to address God as Father! The pagans cowered before their unpredictable and ill-mannered gods. The Jews had Abraham as their father (cf. Jn. 8:53) and recognized the fatherhood of God over their nation (cf. Jer. 31:9), but they did not address Him as Father in personal prayer. We as Christians, however, are adopted into the family of God, "For you did not receive the spirit of bondage again to fear, but you received the Spirit of adoption by whom we cry out, 'Abba, Father'" (Rom. 8:15, also cf. Gal. 4:6). Of this blessing, St. John Chrysostom writes,

> In that one title, those who call God 'Father' confess at once the forgiveness of sins, the adoption, the heirship, the brotherhood, which he has with the Only-begotten, and the gift of the Spirit. For none can call God Father except he who has obtained all these blessings. [141]

When praying and worshiping, we utilize the language given to us in Holy Scripture. As St. John of Damascus teaches,

> It is impossible either to say or fully to understand anything about God beyond what has been divinely proclaimed to us, whether told or

---

[141] St. John Chrysostom, *Catena Aurea, Gospel of St. Matthew* 6.9.

revealed, by the sacred declarations of the Old and New Testaments." [142]

When discussing the study of Scriptures and theology, another saint wrote:

> Since we are to talk about the things of God, let us assume that God has full knowledge of Himself, and bow with humble reverence to His words. For He Whom we can only know through His own words is the fitting witness concerning Himself. [143]

In our culture, there are some people who refuse to refer to God as Father, preferring "mother" or something more gender neutral. However, we cannot change the way God has revealed Himself to us. Doing so is to reconstruct both Christianity and God in the image of something other than what was divinely revealed. Casting God in our own image is idolatry. As a philosopher once said, "In the beginning, God created man in His own image. Since then, man has been returning the favor." [144] In other words, when we do not like something about God or the Christian faith, we are tempted to simply recreate God in our own image so that Christianity can serve our purposes or make us a bit more comfortable. However, the Orthodox Church teaches us to hold fast the divinely revealed truth about God. Such truth

---

[142] St. John of Damascus, *On the Orthodox Faith*, 1.2, p. 168.

[143] St. Hilary of Poitiers, *On the Trinity*, Book 1.18.

[144] A rephrasing of Voltaire, "Si Dieu nous a faits à son image, nous le lui avons bien rendu." From his *Le Sottisier de Voltaire*.

comes from the Holy Scriptures, the Ecumenical Councils, and the consensus of the Church Fathers who help us rightly interpret the Scriptures.

GOD AS SON

The Son knows the Father far more intimately than we ever will. As He said, "I and My Father are one." That does not mean they are the same Person, but that they share the same divinity, "For the entire fullness of God's natures dwells bodily in Christ" (Col. 2:9). Much has already been written about the Son of God in the pages above as well as the chapter entitled "The Cure for Sin and Death," so only a little more will be added here. The Son shares both the essence and the energies of God the Father, but His *hypostasis* (Person) is different. In the Ecumenical Councils, we affirm many truths about the Son of God:

- He is of one essence (consubstantial) with the Father (Council of Nicaea, 325 AD).
- He shares the same essence with the Holy Spirit (First Council of Constantinople, 381 A.D.).
- At His Incarnation, He was born fully God and fully man, and the two natures were united in His one *hypostasis* without any mixing or confusion (Councils of Ephesus, 431 A.D. and Chalcedon, 451 A.D.).
- In His full humanity, He had a human will; in His divinity, He also had a divine will. For each nature (human and divine), there is a will. Like the two natures, the two wills were united in the Person of the God-man Jesus Christ. Our Lord submitted

His human will to the divine will (cf. Matt. 26:39) (Second Council of Constantinople, 680 A.D.).

- Because He was fully man, Jesus Christ our God can be depicted in iconography (just like He could have been photographed if cameras existed back then). His Incarnation sanctified matter, which is why we venerate images of our Lord, the Cross, and even the saints. The latter are venerated because, through the grace of God, the image and likeness of God was restored within them (Second Council of Nicaea, 787 A.D.).

GOD AS HOLY SPIRIT

The third Person of the Holy Trinity is the Holy Spirit (Holy Ghost in some older English translations). The Holy Spirit plays a crucial role in the salvation of every person. St. Paul wrote that those who have the Holy Spirit dwelling in them will have the fruit of the Spirit to show it. Such "fruit of the Spirit is love, joy, peace, longsuffering, kindness, goodness, faithfulness, gentleness, self-control" (Gal. 5:22-23). Through the Holy Spirit, the Church is equipped to carry out its mission to be a hospital for the soul - a place of healing for all humanity. Various gifts and offices given by the Holy Spirit are listed in 1st Corinthians 12.

The indwelling of the Holy Spirit helps us to keep the faith (2 Tim. 1:14). So important is the role of the Spirit in our lives, that St. Seraphim of Sarov stated, "The true aim of our Christian life consists in the acquisition of the Holy Spirit of God."[145] Without the grace of the Holy Spirit, St. Seraphim explained, "no one is or can be saved."[146] He added, "Prayer, fasting, almsgiving, and other good works done for Christ's sake are merely means for acquiring the Spirit of God."[147] We Orthodox Christians should remember the end goal of both asceticism and the virtues is to commune with God in the Holy Spirit. Because life in the Spirit is so important, St. Seraphim told his disciple,

> [You should] always ask yourself: 'Am I in the Spirit of God or not?' And if you are in the Spirit, blessed be God!... But if we are not in the Spirit, we must discover why and for what reason our Lord God the Holy Spirit has willed to abandon us; we must seek Him again through His goodness. And we must attack the enemies that drive us away from Him until even their dust is no more."[148]

To those who attain to such an intimacy with the Holy Spirit, St. Paul writes, "Do you not know that your body is the temple of the Holy Spirit who is in you, whom you have from God, and you are not your own?" (1 Cor. 6:19) So closely are we united to the Holy Spirit that our bodies are no longer considered our own but are sanctified temples of God. In pre-

---

[145] Seraphim of Sarov, "The Acquisition of the Holy Spirit," in *Little Russian Philokalia, Vol. 1*, 79.
[146] Ibid., 82.
[147] Ibid., 80.
[148] Ibid., 87.

modern times, kings marked official documents with a wax seal to show that these documents were of royal legitimacy. Similarly, God seals us with His Holy Spirit (Eph. 4:30) to mark us as His own. That is one reason we must refrain from sinful conduct. Spiritually, we do not want to become like Manasseh who defiled the temple of God and brought judgment upon the Hebrew nation (2 Kgs. 21:1-18).

For most of the Church year, Orthodox services generally begin with the prayer "O Heavenly King," in which we ask the Holy Spirit to "come and abide in us." Prayer and worship begin and end with action of the Holy Spirit within us. Through this sanctifying action of the Spirit, God adopts us as His children, which enables us to refer to God as our Father (cf. Rom. 8:15).

THE PROCESSION OF THE HOLY SPIRIT

While many Christian confessions agree that the Spirit is of the same essence (substance) as the Father and the Son, Orthodox theology emphasizes the personhood of the Holy Spirit. This Spirit is not an impersonal energy or force emanating from God. The Creed, as modified by the Second Ecumenical Council (First Constantinople, 381 A.D.) and affirmed by subsequent Ecumenical Councils, states the Holy Spirit "proceeds from the Father," which is a quote from the Gospel of John:

> But when the Helper comes, whom I shall send to you from the Father, the Spirit of truth who

proceeds from the Father, He will testify of Me
(John 15:26).

While the Son of God sends us the Holy Spirit, the
Spirit's eternal procession is from the Father. Over
the centuries, the Roman Catholic Church modified
the Creed to state the Holy Spirit "proceeds from the
Father *and the Son*" (italics added). This phrase, "and
the Son" or *filioque* in Latin, was added to combat
Arianism in the West. It is foreign to the Eastern
Orthodox Tradition when it comes to the Creed. It can
be justified if the Roman Catholic Church means that
the Holy Spirit is sent to us by the Father and the Son
(cf. John 15:26 above), or if they mean the Holy Spirit
proceeds from the Father *through* the Son.[149] But we
do not confess that the Holy Spirit eternally proceeds
from the Father and the Son, rather, from the Father
alone.[150]

All this may seem like theological hair splitting
for most Christians. However, over the centuries, the
Orthodox Church has made the distinction to protect
the truth about the Holy Spirit in which the Father is
seen as the fountainhead of the Holy Trinity, while
the Son is eternally begotten of Him and the Holy
Spirit eternally proceeds from the Father. The *filioque*

---

[149] Several ancient Orthodox theologians spoke of a
procession from the Father through the Son including
Maximus the Confessor (*Questions to Thalassium*, 63),
Gregory of Nyssa (*Against Eunomius*, 1.36), and Hilary of
Poitiers (*On the Trinity*, 12.55).
[150] For more on this topic, see *Mystagogy of the Holy Spirit* by
St. Photios the Great.

could potentially result in a theology in which the Holy Spirit appears to be in subordination to the Father and Son - or perhaps an impersonal energy (such as love) that emanates from them. That in turn could make it appear He is a lesser deity.

NOT THREE GODS

The title of each Person in the Holy Trinity reveals who they are in relation to the Father. All three Persons are equally divine and eternal, all "are equally uncreated."[151] The Father always was and is Father, as St. Basil wrote, "The God of the universe is Father from infinity; He did not at some point begin to be Father."[152] The Son has always existed as eternally begotten of the Father. These two relational titles are easily understood in English. However, the Spirit's title is less apparent to us. Spirit in both the original biblical languages (*pneuma* in Greek and *ruach* in Hebrew) can mean wind or breath. The Son is called the Word (Greek *logos*) in St. John's Gospel. Since a word (*logos*) cannot be spoken without breath (*pneuma*), we can see in these titles a revelation in the unity and eternality of the Holy Trinity: the Father speaks the Word, which simultaneously includes Breath (Spirit). This trinitarian reality is attested to in Ps. 32:6 (LXX) which states, "By the Word (*logos*) of the Lord the heavens were made, and all the host of them by the Breath (*pneuma*) of His mouth."

---

[151] Gregory of Nyssa, *Against Eunomius*, 2.9.
[152] Basil the Great, *Against Eunomius*, 2.12.

Another useful allegory given for the Holy Trinity in patristic literature is that of the sun. The sun exists with light and heat simultaneously. There was never a time that the sun lacked both light and heat. Yet the light and heat are begotten or proceed from the sun itself.[153] Of course, such allegories have their limitations and can cause confusion if pushed too far. But they teach us that God has always existed in tri-unity.

For some non-Christians, our theology of the Holy Trinity may sound like a soft polytheism. However, that is not the case. As an earthly example, we may see three people: Peter, James, and John.[154] They are building a house together. While they are three persons in one human nature working toward a common goal, all three still have individual (and even competing) wills. In contrast to these three men, the Holy Trinity is three Persons in one divine nature with one will. Likewise, Peter, James, and John may work together, but they inhabit different spaces in the physical realm. In contrast, each Person of the Holy Trinity abides in one another. St. Gregory of Nyssa explains:

> We are not to think of the Father as ever parted from the Son, nor to look for the Son as separate from the Holy Spirit. As it is impossible to 'ascend to the Father,' unless our thoughts are exalted there through the Son, so it is impossible also to

---

[153] Gregory of Nyssa, *Against Eunomius*, 1.36.
[154] This example is adapted from Gregory of Nyssa's *On Not Three Gods: To Ablabius*.

say that 'Jesus is Lord except by the Holy Spirit.' Therefore, Father, Son, and Holy Spirit are to be known only in a perfect Trinity, in closest consequence and union with each other, before all creation, before all the ages, before anything whatever of which we can form an idea. The Father is always Father, and in Him the Son, and with the Son the Holy Spirit.[155]

Some Christians may feel overwhelmed by all these theological details. My purpose here, however, is not to overwhelm but to provide an explanation of what Orthodox Christians mean when we talk about God. God is an infinite mystery that we will progressively know more deeply for all eternity. While certain attributes about God have been divinely revealed to us, no amount of prayer or theological study will ever come close to encompassing or "figuring out" all of God. As St. Gregory the Theologian wisely stated:

> For neither has any one yet breathed the whole air, nor has any mind entirely comprehended, or speech exhaustively contained the Being of God. But we sketch Him by His Attributes, and so obtain a certain faint and feeble and partial idea concerning Him.[156]

---

[155] Gregory of Nyssa, *On the Holy Spirit: Against the Macedonians.*
[156] Gregory of Nazianzus, *Fourth Theological Oration (Oration 30)*, 17.

APPENDIX B: BAPTISM

In the beginning, God created mankind "in His own image" (Gen. 1:27), and looking upon His creation, declared it "very good indeed" (Gen. 1:31). Everything in creation was at peace with God and mankind. But by the third chapter of Genesis, everything changes. Death and corruption enter the material creation. The Apostle Paul recounts this fact,

> Therefore, just as sin entered the world through one man, and death through sin, in this way death spread to all people, because all sinned (Rom. 5:12).

Adam, Eve, and all their posterity would experience death and a strong inclination toward sin. With the introduction of the Law, we became aware of sin, but this awareness did not give us the power to break sin's hold over us (cf. Rom. 7:10-13). Lamenting our sad state, the Apostle again says,

> What a wretched man I am! Who will rescue me from this body of death? Thanks be to God through Jesus Christ our Lord! (Rom. 7:24-25)

"Thanks be to God," indeed, we were not abandoned but have hope in the loving God "who wants everyone to be saved and to come to the knowledge of the truth" (1 Tim. 2:4). At the Incarnation, the Son of God wrapped Himself in flesh and assumed our entire human nature. Jesus Christ was both fully God and fully man. His complete assumption of our human nature made it possible for Him to save us from sin and death.[157] On Holy Friday, He nailed our sins to the Cross and then descended into the grave - freeing us from the bondage of sin. After setting Hade's captives free, He raised Himself from the dead on Pascha (Easter Sunday) - defeating death. He then showed His resurrected and glorified body to over five hundred witnesses (1 Cor. 15:6) - displaying His victory. Forty days after His resurrection, He ascended in glory to seat our glorified and deified human nature at the right hand of God. Through baptism and life in the Church, we participate with our Lord in this story of salvation.

Though we can begin our Christ-life now, our victory over sin and death is not presently obvious. Ancestral sin is inherited by us from Adam at birth, which means we all experience an inclination toward sin, physical decay (e.g., disease and sickness), and death. But when we are baptized, we are "born again" (John 3:3, 1 Pet. 1:23), forgiven our sins, and made members of the kingdom of heaven. As St. Gregory

---

[157] See St. Gregory the Theologian's Epistle 101, *To Cledonius the Priest Against Apollinarius.*

Palamas wrote, "Holy baptism is the gate leading those being baptized into heaven."[158]

This heavenly second birth is much more than an outward sign of our faith in Christ. It plants the seed of grace within our hearts, creating an actual change within us. We are cleansed from the curse of the ancestral sin; we put on the divine Christ, "For as many of you as were baptized into Christ have put on Christ" (Gal. 3:27); we enter into His death, "Or do you not know that as many of us as were baptized into Christ Jesus were baptized into His death?" (Rom. 6:3); so that we can enter into His life, for "if we died with Christ, we believe that we shall also live with Him" (Rom. 6:8). While our entrance into this immortal and incorruptible life is not yet fully evident, we accept with faith that in baptism we "died, and [our] life is hidden with Christ in God" (Col. 3:3). Until the day that the hidden life in Christ is revealed,

> the whole creation groans and labors with birth pangs together until now. Not only that, but we also who have the firstfruits of the Spirit, even we ourselves groan within ourselves, eagerly waiting for the adoption, the redemption of our body (Rom. 8:22-23).

The change brought about within us through faith and baptism grants us the grace and power

---

[158] Gregory Palamas, *The Homilies*, 60.

needed to make progress in the spiritual life. The Apostle Paul states to each Christian,

> Put off, concerning your former conduct, the old man which grows corrupt according to the deceitful lusts, and be renewed in the spirit of your mind (Eph. 4:22-23).

This renewal of the mind includes a strengthening of the will to fulfill the commandments of the Gospel and to live a life that is appropriate to a person abiding in the glorified humanity of Christ, sometimes called the new man, "Put on the new man which was created according to God, in true righteousness and holiness" (Eph. 4:24).

In this manner, the baptized Christian is no longer a slave to sin and the ways of death but an adopted son of God. The baptism service confirms this new life and identity,

> But do thou, O Master of all, show this water to be the water of redemption, the water of sanctification, the purification of flesh and spirit, the loosing of bonds, the remission of sins, the illumination of the soul, the laver of regeneration, the renewal of the Spirit, the gift of adoption to sonship, the garment of incorruption, the fountain of life.[159]

Not a Magic Trick

The sacrament of baptism, like all the sacraments, is not magical. What that means is that it

---

[159] Hapgood, *Service Book*, 279.

cannot be separated from the ascetical and virtuous life established by the Church. Without living in accordance with the Church's teachings, partaking of the sacraments is little more than superstition.

After baptism, we will continue to struggle against sin. However, the grace we receive in baptism prepares us for spiritual combat and can prevent sin from having the upper hand in the fight. As we struggle, our free will is healed so that we begin to desire the things of God rather than sin.

The sixth chapter of Romans discusses this transformation from being slaves of sin into slaves of God. The Apostle Paul writes, "Consider yourselves dead to sin and alive to God in Christ Jesus...Do not let sin reign in your mortal body so that you obey its desires" (Rom. 6:11-12). These words "consider" and "do not let" imply we must still exert effort. But in doing so, we transform our "mortal bodies" from being "weapons for unrighteousness" into "weapons for righteousness" (Rom. 6:13). Contrary to worldly wisdom which tends toward a dualistic perspective that belittles the role of the body, our baptized body is used in spiritual combat to aid us against the enemy. Through a life of participation in the sacraments and asceticism, we take up arms against our spiritual foe.

St. John of Damascus writes, "By baptism, then, remission of sins is granted to all alike, but the grace of the Spirit is granted in proportion to the faith and the previous purification."[160] In other words, all

---

[160] John of Damascus, *On the Orthodox Faith*, 346.

receive forgiveness in the font, but the grace bestowed upon each person differs depending on the depth of their faith and how much they have struggled toward purity in preparation for baptism. Adults who wish to receive the grace of God through the sacraments must struggle to live in accordance with the commandments of Christ and the teachings of the Church. For infants, young children, and the intellectually impaired, the faith of their godparents or parents who bring them to baptism and to the chalice helps bring about the grace of God. It is similar to the Gospel passage in which the faith of the friends of the paralyzed man brought about the man's healing. The Scripture states, "When Jesus saw their faith, He said to the paralytic, 'Son, be of good cheer; your sins are forgiven you'" (Matt. 9:2). Note the plural "their faith," not "his faith."

This story in the scripture is seen by some Fathers as an image of baptism. St. Gregory Palamas, paraphrasing our Lord, writes,

> 'Son, be of good cheer…Set aside your anxiety over your sins, for they are forgiven. Forget your horror at the sufferings which threaten you, for you will inherit the promises, seeing you have become My child and heir.' In practice this happens through holy baptism, when we are born again through the Spirit of adoption (Rom. 8:15), receiving forgiveness of our former sin, and becoming heirs of God according to the promise (Gal. 3:29), and joint heirs with Christ (Rom. 8:17)… Strengthened by the grace and power of holy baptism within us, we become vigorous and active in virtue, and

bring into subjection our mental and physical capabilities and those material things which ought to be subservient to them, but which formerly overpowered us. We then go wherever pleases God and ourselves and, as far as we can, move to our real home, the eternal heavenly mansions.[161]

In synergy, we work together with our Lord and His Holy Spirit dwelling within us, strengthening us for the spiritual struggle ahead. These salvific struggles renew the image of God within us and bring us into His likeness.

The Form of Baptism

There are certain key components present in every Orthodox baptism. This form is part of the ancient Church tradition.

TRINITARIAN

Baptisms in the Orthodox Church are completed "In the name of the Father, and of the Son, and of the Holy Spirit," with a complete immersion in the water following each divine name. Therefore, there are a total of three immersions. Aside from the Orthodox, there are few Christians who practice such a baptism.

As we can see from reading the Acts of the Apostles, there were two types of baptism which devout, God-fearing Jews of the first century commonly received. The initial one was the "Baptism of John" (cf. Acts 13:24, 18:25, 19:3), which was an outward sign of repentance, which could perhaps be

---

[161] St. Gregory Palamas, *The Homilies*, 29.7.

compared to the sprinkling of ashes on the head at the beginning of Lent in some Western Christian confessions. It does not forgive sins or grant salvation to a person, but it is a sign of devotion and a desire to "get right" with God. The second type of baptism was the "Baptism of Jesus" or "Baptism in the name of Jesus" (Acts 2:38, 8:12, 19:5). This baptism is the one we presently practice. It is for the remission of sins and everlasting life. The Baptism of Jesus is not in Jesus' name only. Rather, it follows the formula given by Jesus to the Apostles when He said, *Baptizing them in the name of the Father and of the Son and of the Holy Spirit* (Matt. 28:19).

Some Unitarian groups insist that the mentioning of baptism in Jesus' name throughout the Acts of the Apostles is proof that such a practice is the most original form of Christian baptism. However, there is simply no historical evidence to affirm that early Christians disregarded our Lord's command in Matthew 28:19. On the contrary, ancient Christian extrabiblical documents affirm Trinitarian baptism. As one Protestant commentary states,

> We are not to suppose that any other formula was used than that prescribed by our Lord (Matthew 28:19). But as baptism was preceded by a confession of faith similar to that in our own Baptismal Service, so it was a true description to speak of baptism as being in the Name of Jesus Christ.[162]

---

[162] *Pulpit Commentary*, Acts 8:16, online edition.

FULL IMMERSION

Our English word "baptize" is a transliteration of the Greek word βαπτίζω (*baptizo*), which literally means to immerse or submerge. Therefore, from the time of the Apostles to the present day, the Orthodox Church fully submerges the one being baptized. The Apostle Paul alludes to this when he writes, "All were baptized into Moses in the cloud and in the sea" (1 Cor. 10:2). The crossing of the Red Sea was below sea level, with walls of water on either side of them (Ex. 14:22). So, the Hebrews walked "under" the sea, with towering walls of water on either side of them. Additionally, the form of immersive baptism was a Jewish form that Christians inherited with a new meaning and grace. When our Lord Himself was baptized by John the Forerunner, the Scripture shows that He was immersed, for He had to come up out of the water, "When He had been baptized, Jesus came up immediately from the water" (Matt. 3:16). Numerous ancient Christian accounts, such as *The Didache*, refer to baptism as immersion.

The Didache was an early Christian document, dating sometime between the era of the Apostles and 150 AD. Regardless of the exact date, it is one of the oldest non-biblical extent works referencing aspects of early Church oral tradition. In its chapter on baptism, the anonymous author writes,

> Baptize into the name of the Father, and of the Son, and of the Holy Spirit, in living water. But if you have no living water, baptize into other water; and if you cannot do so in cold water, do so in warm.

143

> But if you have neither, pour out water three times
> upon the head into the name of Father and Son and
> Holy Spirit (Chapter 7).

The Didache clearly demonstrates the early tradition of immersive baptism in "living water."[163] The mention of pouring water upon the head as an exception to the rule implies that immersion was the rule. Additionally, the three pourings with the name of the Trinity imply that immersions would have likewise been threefold. A second century witness named St. Justin Martyr wrote,

> Then they [the catechumens] are brought by us
> where there is water, and are regenerated in the
> same manner in which we were ourselves
> regenerated. For, in the name of God, the Father
> and Lord of the universe, and our Savior Jesus
> Christ, and of the Holy Spirit, they then receive the
> washing with water. For Christ also said, 'Except
> ye be born again, ye shall not enter into the
> kingdom of heaven.' [164]

Infant Baptism

While the Orthodox Church offers baptism to everyone from their infancy onward, many Christian confessions do not baptize anyone until they are old enough to decide that they want to be a follower of Christ. In Protestantism, baptism follows "asking

---

[163] Living water simply meant running water such as a river. In this way, Christian baptism emulated our Lord's baptism in the Jordan River.
[164] Justin Martyr, *First Apology*, 61.

Jesus into your heart." It is, in that sense, an outward proclamation of the decision to become a Christian. For many of these Christians, the sacrament conveys no grace; it is merely an act of obedience to Christ's command in the Great Commission (Matt. 28:19-20). Therefore, Protestant Christians tend to be critical of the traditional practice of baptizing infants. For Orthodox converts coming from a Protestant background, it may be helpful to explain why we Orthodox baptize infants. The following pages will show that our practice is historically, scripturally, and theologically correct.

BIBLICAL SURVEY

Neither in the New Testament, nor in the earliest records of Christian history, is the discussion of a minimum baptismal age raised. In the Great Commission, our Lord commands his Apostles to, "Go therefore and make disciples of all the nations, baptizing them in the name of the Father and of the Son and of the Holy Spirit" (Matt. 28:19), giving no minimum age requirements.

Shortly after the Ascension, when the crowd gathers around the Apostles on Pentecost, Peter addresses them saying, "Repent, and let every one of you be baptized in the name of Jesus Christ for the remission of sins; and you shall receive the gift of the Holy Spirit" (Acts 2:38). Throughout Acts, many baptisms are recorded. In Acts 10:44-48, the centurion Cornelius and those with him are baptized, which insinuates his entire household was baptized. In Lydia's case, the Scripture explicitly states, "And when she and her household were baptized..." without making any exceptions for age (Acts 16:15).

In one of his epistles, Paul mentions, "Yes, I also baptized the household of Stephanas," (1 Cor. 1:16), which, again, makes no discrimination regarding age. Later in the same epistle, when explaining the crossing of the Red Sea as a typological prefiguration of baptism, Paul writes of the Hebrews, "All were baptized into Moses in the cloud and in the sea" (1 Cor. 10:2), which included men, women, children, and infants.

BAPTISMS IN THE EARLY CHURCH

Aside from the New Testament, several documents have survived from the first generations of Christians. The authors from this era are often called the Apostolic Fathers. Among these men who knew the Apostles and were direct transmitters of the Apostolic Tradition are Saints Ignatius of Antioch, Clement of Rome, and Polycarp of Smyrna.

The latter, St. Polycarp, had a disciple named St. Irenaeus of Lyons who was sent to Gaul (modern-day France). His writings have been translated into English, with the most famous one being *Against Heresies*.[165] Regarding baptism, Irenaeus wrote,

> For He [Christ] came to **save all** through means of Himself – **all**, I say, who through Him are **born**

---

[165] Its original title was *A Refutation and Subversion of Knowledge Falsely So Called*

again to God – **infants**, and **children**, and boys, and youths, and old men.*166*

His statement could not be clearer: those who were being *born again* included *all*, from *infants* to *old men*. Scriptural commentaries - from the earliest centuries until today - consistently interpreted the passage "Ye must be born again" (John 3:7) to refer to baptism, so there is no doubt among scholars or Christians that Irenaeus was referring to infant baptism in the primitive Church. The practice was so well-accepted, that in St. Irenaeus' book refuting various theological errors, infant baptism is mentioned in passing. There are no polemics surrounding the topic nor any hint of dissenting opinions. It has been an ordinary, everyday part of life in the Church since the first centuries.[167]

WHY BAPTIZE INFANTS?

One day, when the usual crowd surrounded our Lord Jesus, the people began sending their children to

---

[166] St. Irenaeus of Lyons, *Against Heresies* (Chap. 22.4), 391.

[167] I will concede that during the third century there arose a practice of waiting until the deathbed to receive baptism (St. Constantine the Great famously did that). This practice came from the erroneous opinion that serious sins could not be forgiven after baptism. Consequently, some people chose to wait until the end of their life - especially if they were involved in war or politics. Such an idea was never fully embraced by the Church. St. Gregory the Theologian wrote against this practice in his *Oration 40*, which indicates people were continuing to delay baptism up until the fourth century.

Him to be blessed by Him. The disciples did not want to see Christ bothered with children, so they rebuked them. However, our Lord responded, "Let the little children come to Me, and do not forbid them; for of such is the kingdom of heaven" (Matt. 19:14). God wants every person of every age to be allowed access to Him. We firmly believe in the Orthodox Church that our sacraments are encounters with God: they unite us to Him. What parent would not want their child to encounter Christ and to be blessed by Him? Additionally, the infant mortality rate was much higher in those times. Nobody wanted their child to die without becoming a member of the Church, so infants, especially those born sickly, were baptized.

ORIGINAL SIN AND SINLESS BABIES

Because baptism washes away sin, some people struggle with why we would baptize infants and young children who carry no guilt of sin within them. The Lord through the Prophet Ezekiel taught that every person will be responsible for his own sins. The entire eighteenth chapter in his book of prophecy is dedicated to this theme, but it can be summarized in one verse, "The soul who sins shall die. The son shall not bear the wrongdoing of his father, nor shall the father bear the wrongdoing of his son" (18:20). Every person is responsible for the guilt of his or her own sins.

Yet children are certainly not free from the effects of sin in human nature, which is why we baptize them. Perhaps the easiest way to explain the transmission of the effects of sin - without its guilt - is to consider congenital diseases. Many of these diseases are hereditary while others come from external factors such as a mother's substance use. A baby born with congenital defects has committed no sin nor has it made a single wrong choice, yet it must suffer the consequences of conditions that existed before its birth.

When we die and are reborn in the sacrament of baptism, we are putting off "the old man," (cf. Eph. 4:22, Col. 3:9) which is a metaphor for the old, sin-inclined human nature,

> Our old man was crucified with Him, that the body of sin might be done away with, that we should no longer be slaves of sin. For he who has died has been freed from sin. Now if we died with Christ, we believe that we shall also live with Him (Rom. 6:6-8).

This death and life in Christ as well as the adoption into the kingdom of God are what we want our children to receive. No, they are not capable of making an independent decision to follow Christ in infancy, but they also did not choose to be born into a damaged human nature infected with the diseases of sin and death. At the very least, these little Christians will begin to receive the grace of God and the healing of their human nature which is bestowed upon them through the grace-filled sacraments of our Church. They will be baptized, chrismated, and begin receiving the precious Body and Blood of our Lord so they may have a fighting chance against the diabolical schemes that will soon be launched against them.

They have been born amid a great spiritual war, and we are doing everything possible to protect and save them.

APPENDIX C: WHY DID CHRIST DIE ON THE CROSS?

G rowing up as an Evangelical Protestant, the emphasis that I heard in most hymns and sermons was on the salvific sacrifice of Christ upon the cross – He died in our place to appease the wrath of God. Now our sins are forgiven, and we can go to heaven when we die. These ideas come from various atonement theories, of which Penal Substitutionary Atonement (PSA) is one of the most influential.

In this chapter, we will explore how the over emphasis upon atonement theories unintentionally misrepresents both God and the Christian faith. Since many of us in Western culture have been indoctrinated with atonement theories, it can be difficult to mentally disentangle their theology from Scriptural images of ransom, propitiation, and debt satisfaction. The following pages will address how we can understand such scriptural imagery without distorting the character of God.

SUBSTITUTIONARY ATONEMENT

First, we should define Penal Substitutionary Atonement. It can be explained by imagining a cosmic scale that represents divine justice. Mankind was created sinless but then sinned against God, causing the scale of justice to become imbalanced. The imbalance caused a rift between God and humanity that was impossible for humanity to heal - for all of mankind inherited Adam's guilt and sin, and no human effort could reverse that. This rift caused God to look upon humanity with wrath.[168] Though He wanted to draw close to humanity, God was prevented by His justice, wrath, and offended honor.

Since it was impossible for humanity to correct the wrong, God sent His only-begotten Son who willingly died as a substitute for us. He took our penalties of torment and death upon the Cross. He was a perfect, spotless sacrifice, and therefore only He could balance the cosmic scale of divine justice. Josh McDowell, a popular Protestant apologist, takes this concept to its logical conclusion. He writes that Jesus not only died for us humans but also "for God

---

[168] Perhaps nobody spoke more about the wrath of God than the fiery Jonathan Edwards. "Sinners in the Hands of an Angry God" is one of his well-known sermons.

the Father."[169] God wanted to draw close to us but could not; He was hindered by the force of justice. Therefore, Jesus had to die for the Father as well. Through the Son's sacrificial death, the Father imputes the Son's righteousness upon us – hiding our corruption and sin under Jesus Christ who covers us. This divine covering enables the Father to be with us.

PROBLEMS WITH PSA

Some of the problems with this theological concept include the following:

1.   Introducing divine justice as a force more powerful than God is problematic. Anything that can bind God or force Him to take certain actions is inherently greater than God. To avoid polytheism, it is necessary for proponents of this system to attribute this limiting or binding force to the divine nature.

2.   However, attributing this binding divine justice to God's nature presents another problem. If God wants to be close to us but cannot because of His inherent justice or offended honor, then it presents *a* "schism in the very idea of God."[170] God wants something but another part of Him refuses it. Truthfully, there are no opposing thoughts or attributes within God - one aspect desiring love and mercy, the other binding Him to nearly insatiable justice. God is not like fallen humanity with

---

[169] *More than a Carpenter*, Josh McDowell, Tyndale House, 2005, pg. 110.
[170] George MacDonald, *Unspoken Sermons Vol. 3*, Justice

conflicting desires or energies. He is whole and completely unified in will and activity. There cannot be competing or opposing desires within Him.

3.   The idea that justice can be achieved through the torment and death of innocent victims is irrational. It is unjust to punish innocent people. Even though our Lord was willing to be sacrificed, how does the persecution of the innocent correct an imbalance in divine justice? It only imbalances it further. Any human judge who gave the death sentence to an innocent child in place of a convicted murderer would be called wicked and unjust – even if the child were willing to go along with the plan. It is even worse if we assume God *needs* this sort of injustice to gratify some sort of divine desire. As the old saying goes, "Two wrongs don't make a right."

4.   This system, as developed by Anselm of Canterbury and Protestant Reformers, places the problem upon God. Many humans would be content to merely live and die. But because our sins offended His honor and sense of justice, we are bound for an eternity of torment in hell. In this system, God needs to be saved from an irrational sense of justice and we need to be saved from God. But God is "good and the lover of mankind"[171] - not a cruel avenger. While we certainly need to be saved, it is not salvation *from* God that we need but *in* God. For God Himself is our haven of salvation (cf. Ps. 144:2).

5.   Divine justice in substitutionary atonement theories requires payment. In this system, there is no

---

[171] A phrase we use often in the Orthodox Divine Liturgy.

forgiveness possible in God's nature without payment.[172] Yet it is possible - even for unbelieving men - to forgive one another for grievances without demanding any form of payment. A sincere apology can reunite two men who have hated one another for years, more so than any great sum of money. Repentance and forgiveness do more to heal and restore relationships than any kind of payment. Therefore, according to this atonement theory, men are naturally more capable of forgiveness and mercy than God is, for we are sometimes capable of restoration without any material exchange. Why do we assume God is any different? He requires us to forgive one another (Matt. 6:15, 18:21-35) without desiring revenge or satisfaction. We are given this command by God to forgive and love unconditionally so that we may be like He is – not because we are better than He is. God is not interested in payments anyway. Rather, He desires a loving union with us.

6.   While God's activities among humanity have varied, God Himself never undergoes any change. Yet if God had a need (unsatisfied justice or offended honor) that required satisfaction, then that means there is something changeable within God. We, as slowly dying organisms, have needs and undergo change. Our sinful state also causes change in our emotions and mental state of being. But the divine nature is not like that.[173] As God said through the

---

[172] MacDowell, *More than a Carpenter*, pp. 111-112.

[173] I emphasize the "divine nature" because our Lord Jesus, in His humanity, did undergo the "blameless passions" such as

Prophet Malachi, "For I am the LORD, I do not change" (Mal. 3:6); for God is "the same yesterday and today and forever" (Heb. 13:8).

7.   Lastly, this system places salvation outside of us and requires nothing from humanity except an acknowledgment of the system itself. It saves us from hell by imputing God's righteousness to us. But there is little need on our part to be transformed into children of God in this life. In the words of George MacDonald,

> The salvation of Christ is salvation from the smallest tendency or leaning to sin. It is a deliverance into the pure air of God's ways of thinking and feeling. It is a salvation that makes the heart pure, with the will and choice of the heart to be pure. To such a heart, sin is disgusting. It sees a thing as it is – that is, as God sees it, for God sees everything as it is. The soul thus saved would rather sink into the flames of hell than steal into heaven and skulk there under the shadow of an imputed righteousness. No soul is saved that would not prefer hell to sin.[174]

This strongly worded statement emphasizes sin as separation from God's love, and that hell is preferable to such separation. The soul that loves God – and knows His love – has a will that is healed and purified. Such a soul would rather be in the fires of hell with

---

need for food, sleep, and even mourning at his friend's funeral (Jn. 11:35).

[174] George MacDonald, *Unspoken Sermons Vol. 3*, Justice, 1889.

the internal comfort of God's love than abide in a heavenly paradise with a love for sin still separating him from God. Ultimately, love for God is heaven while love for sin is hell. These atonement theories generally do not require interior change and healing since the salvation of God is imputed to us, happening as a mostly-external process.

SEARCHING FOR A BETTER ANSWER

For those who have been raised with these atonement theories - who struggled to understand God's love in contrast to His strange thirst for justice - the Orthodox way will be a godsend. In summary, we Orthodox believe that salvation is something that changes us from the inside. It is not something merely external, nor is it imputed upon us. God inhabits the human heart, restoring His image within us, causing an interior change that turns us into precious vessels of the Holy Spirit. We walk in obedience to God's commandments, which further purifies the heart so that we can see God (cf. Matt. 5:8) *as He is* (1 Jn. 3:2). By *seeing*, we mean deep communion with God, knowing Him – not merely gazing upon Him.

Yet the Orthodox answer may leave Orthodox converts with several questions. If Christ did not die to appease the wrath of His Father or to balance the scale of justice, then what was the purpose of His death? Could He have saved us without dying? Also, why do we see language about debt satisfaction and ransom in both Holy Scripture and the Orthodox Church hymns?

Holy Tradition (which includes the Scriptures) makes it clear that Christ's death upon the Cross satisfies a debt that needed to be paid and saves us from sin and death. But how do we separate biblical and patristic language of ransoms and debt satisfaction from images of a God who is bound by justice?

The prior pages were deconstructive; tearing down an erroneous understanding of salvation. The remainder of this chapter will focus on reconstructing a biblical and patristic view of salvation. I will begin mostly without commentary and then tie it together near the end.

BIBLICAL PASSAGES

Several scriptural passages can be referenced that support Christ's death as a ransom, paying a penalty, or as a substitute. These texts are frequently used to defend Penal Substitutionary Atonement. Emphasis in quoted texts throughout this chapter is mine.

> For the Son of man also came not to be served but to serve, and to *give his life as a ransom* for many (Matt. 20:28, Mark 10:45).

> You know that *you were ransomed* from the futile ways inherited from your fathers, not with perishable things such as silver or gold, but *with the precious blood of Christ*, like that of a lamb without blemish or spot (1 Pet. 1:18-19).

He himself *bore our sins in his body* on the tree, that we might die to sin and live to righteousness. *By his wounds you have been healed* (1 Pet. 2:24).

But as it is, he has appeared once for all at the end of the age to *put away sin by the sacrifice of himself* (Heb. 9:26).

Since, therefore, we are now *justified by his blood*, much more shall we be saved by him from the wrath of God. For if while we were enemies we were *reconciled to God* by the death of his Son, much more, now that we are reconciled, shall we be saved by his life (Rom. 5:9-10).

They are *justified by his grace as a gift,* through the redemption which is in Christ Jesus, whom God put forward *as an expiation [propitiation] by his blood*, to be received by faith (Rom. 3:24-25).

He is the *expiation [propitiation] for our sins*, and not for ours only but also for the sins of the whole world (1 Jn. 2:2)

EARLY CHURCH PASSAGES

EPISTLE OF MATHETES (AD 120-130): Probably the earliest hint of ransom theology outside of the Bible comes from the *Epistle of Mathetes to Diognetus*, who was a "disciple of the Apostles." Mathetes writes,

He Himself took on Him the burden of our iniquities, *He gave His own Son as a ransom for us*, the holy One for transgressors, the blameless One for the wicked...For what other thing was capable

159

of covering our sins than His righteousness? By what other one was it possible that we, the wicked and ungodly, could be justified, than by the only Son of God? *O sweet exchange!* O unsearchable operation![175]

However, in the early years of the Church, there was no hint of the Son trying to appease God's wrath. Quite the opposite! Mathetes writes,

God...proved Himself not merely a friend of mankind, but also long-suffering. Yes, He was always of such a character, and still is, and will ever be, kind and good, and *free from wrath.*[176]

Here, Mathetes affirms substitution and ransom imagery, yet denies any wrath or changeable condition in God.

ST. AUGUSTINE (†430): The fifth-century bishop of Hippo continues the theme of our being saved from death and the devil through Christ's death:

For whereas *by His death the one and most real sacrifice was offered up for us,* whatever fault there was, whence principalities and powers held us fast as of right *to pay its penalty,* He cleansed, abolished, extinguished; and by His own resurrection He also called us...The nations acknowledge and with pious humility imbibe *the price paid for themselves,*

---

[175] *Epistle of Mathetes to Diognetus*, Chapter IX, Ante-Nicene Fathers, Vol. 1, pg. 28.
[176] Ibid., chapter VIII.

and in trust upon it abandon their enemy, and gather together to their Redeemer.[177]

ST. SYMEON THE NEW THEOLOGIAN (†1022): St. Symeon refers to Christ's death on the Cross as a sacrifice that He offered to God as a substitute for us,

> Thus God, Who is incomparably higher than the whole visible and invisible creation, accepted human nature, which is higher than the whole visible creation, and *offered it as a sacrifice to His God and Father*. Being shamed by such a sacrifice (I speak thus), and honoring it, the Father could not leave it in the hands of death. Therefore He annihilated His sentence and, first of all and at the beginning, resurrected from the dead Him Who had given Himself as a *sacrifice as a redemption and as a substitute for men* who are of the same race as Himself.[178]

OTHER FATHERS: In the Divine Liturgy of St. Basil, the priest prays, "He gave himself as a ransom to death, in which we were held captive, sold under sin."[179] Additionally, St. Gregory of Nyssa in his *Great Catechism* and Origen in his *Commentary on Matthew* also utilize ransom imagery.[180]

In all the writings that I searched from the first one thousand years of Church history, not much

---

[177] *On the Trinity*, Book 4, Chapter 17, NPNF Series 1 Vol. 3.
[178] St. Symeon the New Theologian, *The First-Created Man,* St. Herman of Alaska Brotherhood, 2013, pp. 47-48.
[179] A prayer from the Holy Anaphora. *Hieratikon, Vol. 2.* St. Tikhon's Monastery Press, 2017, pg. 183.
[180] Nyssa, *Great Catechism*, 2.23; Origen, *Commentary on Matthew*, Book 12.28.

significance is attributed to ransom or debt payment imagery other than an occasional mention. In the Christian East, the emphasis in God's salvific work was almost always upon the restoration and healing of human nature.

PATRISTIC FINE-TUNING

St. Gregory the Theologian of Nazianzen (†390) was quick to point out that language about ransoms and debts being paid is not wrong but should not be stretched too far. By our sins, we made ourselves slaves of the devil and captives of death. However, neither death nor the devil had any real legal rights over us. It is not as if God, wanting us back, realized He owed the devil a great sum to legally retrieve us. The devil himself owes his existence to God and is perpetually indebted to God for that. It is impossible for God to ever owe anyone anything, for "every good gift and every perfect gift is from above, coming down from the Father of lights" (Jam. 1:17), which includes every creature's existence, "for in Him we live and move and have our being" (Acts 17:28) and "by Him all things are held together" (Col. 1:17).

St. Gregory addresses whom Christ died for and how the ransom was paid in a sermon that outlines the Orthodox position quite clearly. He writes:

> *To Whom was that Blood offered* that was shed for us, and why was It shed?... We were detained in bondage by the Evil One, sold under sin, and receiving pleasure in exchange for wickedness. Now, since a ransom belongs only to him who holds in bondage, I ask to whom was this offered,

and for what cause? *If to the Evil One, fie upon the outrage!* If the robber receives ransom, not only from God, but a ransom which consists of God Himself, and has such an illustrious payment for his tyranny, a payment for whose sake it would have been right for him to have left us alone altogether.

In other words, St. Gregory is stating that it is ridiculous to believe that the devil could ever receive God Himself as a ransom payment. By receiving the precious Blood of Christ, the devil would receive a ransom worth far more than all humanity. Perhaps then the ransom was paid to the Father? Gregory continues:

> But if [payment is made] to the Father, I ask first, how? For it was not by Him that we were being oppressed. Next, on what principle did the Blood of His Only begotten Son delight the Father, Who would not receive even Isaac, when he was being offered by his father, but changed the sacrifice, putting a ram in the place of the human victim? Is it not evident that *the Father accepts Him, but neither asked for Him nor demanded Him*? But on account of the Incarnation, and *because Humanity must be sanctified by the Humanity of God*. By that, He delivers us Himself, overcomes the tyrant, and draws us to Himself by the mediation of His Son. He also arranged this to the honor of the Father, Whom it is manifest that He obeys in all things. So much we have said of Christ; the greater part of

what we might say shall be reverenced with silence.[181]

Though we were oppressed sin and death, God owes the devil nothing. Additionally, God is not oppressing us either. There is no imagery of a wrathful God requiring payment in St. Gregory. Quite the opposite. God "neither asked for Him nor demanded Him."

WHY THE SACRIFICIAL LANGUAGE?

If God did not *really* owe anyone anything, why do we find all this language about ransoms and debts being paid? Why sacrifice Christ on the Cross at all if *the Father neither asked for Him nor demanded Him*, and *it was not by [the Father] that we were being oppressed,* according to St. Gregory? To those questions, I propose the following resolutions:

UNDERSTANDING IMAGERY. First, when speaking of spiritual things, we must remember that human language is subpar in expressing what God has done for us. Frequently, Scripture uses imagery to convey concepts, and allegorical imagery should not be pushed too far. For example, St. Paul writes, "You are not your own...you were bought at a price" (1 Cor. 6:19-20). It is not as if God lost ownership of humanity and had to enter a contract with someone to buy us back. The language expresses a reality – that Christ's precious blood purchased and redeemed us – but not in a way that humans make purchases or save

---

[181]Gregory of Nazianzen, *Oration 45: Second Oration on Easter*, Chapter XXII.

captives through ransom payments. The Scriptures were written by ancient Near Eastern people who frequently expressed themselves in metaphor, allegory, hyperbole, and other ways that are less common to modern, Western minds. While these ancients would rightfully assert their imagery is true, what is not always true is the conclusions we draw from systematizing their imagery in a literal way.

HELD BY SIN, DEATH, AND THE DEVIL. With the above said, we understand that through our sin, we metaphorically sold ourselves to death, "for the wages of sin is death" (Rom. 6:23). We were "enslaved to sin" (Rom. 6:6, cf. John 8:34). But God ransomed us from death and sin even though those things have no true ontology or personhood. Sin and death are not actual beings to whom a real ransom can be paid. In Church writings and hymns, we see death and the grave given anthropomorphic attributes (e.g., "Where, O death, is thy sting?," 1 Cor. 15:55); but again, we do not stretch these ideas too far. The devil, on the other hand, is a real being. Yet ransoms paid to him must be understood allegorically since the all-powerful Creator of the cosmos can never be indebted to anyone - as we established above.

SACRIFICE WAS THE WAY OF JEWS AND PAGANS. A sacrifice in the ancient mind was the only way to reconcile humanity to a deity - whether one was a Jew or Gentile. Christianity would have appealed to almost no one if some sacrifice had not been made to set humanity right with divinity. Such a mindset is foreign to us living in a post-Christian society, but it was universal in the ancient world. The author of the epistle to the Hebrews struggled to appease the Jewish conscience. He explained Temple sacrifices were no longer needed, though they still occurred during the early Christian era. Hebrews states,

> According to the Law, almost everything is purified with blood, and without the shedding of blood there is no forgiveness...[But] it is impossible for the blood of bulls and goats to take away sins...But this man [Jesus], after offering one sacrifice for sins forever, sat down at the right hand of God (Heb. 9:22, 10:4,12).

GOD WANTED TO SHOW HIS INCONCEIVABLE LOVE FOR US. If God had simply shown up - uniting human nature to the divine nature - ontologically raising it from the mire of sin and death, it would not have made much of an impression on us. Our Lord Himself said, "Greater love hath no man than this, that a man lay down his life for his friends" (Jn. 15:13). So, a man of great love lays down his life for his friends. But Christ – being the God-man – goes even further. He laid down His life for His enemies, for those of us who had not yet come to obedience (cf. Rom. 5:10, Jn. 15:14). The entire passion drama was for our sakes, to prove how much He loves us, and not from any necessity in God. In other words, God did not need it, but we needed it to understand His extravagant love more deeply.

CHRIST DESIRED TO JOIN US IN DEATH. Fully entering the darkest abyss of the human experience, Christ willingly took upon Himself a publicly disgraceful death, betrayed and abandoned by His earthly friends whom He loved. Elevated into the air, in a position between earth and heaven, His arms were outstretched embracing the entire world. In this elevated position between earth and heaven, He revealed Himself as our way to the heavenly Father.[182] Then He entered the realm of the dead, invading it like a great military general, setting the captives free and conquering the realm that seemed beyond the reach of even the greatest pagan gods.

WE FIRST NEEDED TO BE RAISED FROM THE SUB-NATURAL MAN TO THE NATURAL MAN. Mankind was created in the image and likeness of God, in complete communion with God, and clothed in divine glory. To be a natural human is to be all those things. However, we fell from being in a state *according to nature* to being sub-natural or *contrary to nature*. The nakedness of Adam and Eve was the loss of their natural "clothing" of God's glory. Instead, they were clothed in a state of death and corruption, which Scripture calls "garments of skin" (Gen. 3:21). This is also what the Apostle Paul is referring to when he uses the word, "flesh," such as when he says, "those who are in the flesh cannot please God" (Rom. 8:8) and "flesh and blood cannot inherit the kingdom of God; nor does corruption inherit incorruption" (1 Cor. 15:50). Adam's original sin corrupted our humanity, bringing it to a sub-natural state. The sub-

---

[182] The symbolic beauty of the Incarnation and the Cross are eloquently discussed by St. Athanasius in his work *On the Incarnation*.

natural *flesh* makes full communion with God imposs-ible. However, our Lord's death and resurrection redeemed our humanity from sin and death (acting as a ransom, in some sense), restoring the potential for us to attain to a natural, pre-fallen state.

CHRIST AS THE VICTORIOUS LEADER INTO LIFE ABOVE NATURE. Christ rose from the dead and was the first human to defy death and show that it had no lasting victory over us. Not content to merely right the wrong, to bring humanity from its sub-natural state of death to a natural state free from death, Christ preserved His resurrected human body. At the ascension, He seated human nature at the right hand of God in the heavens (Mark 16:19, Luke 22:69, Acts 7:55, etc.), interceding on our behalf, "For there is one God and one Mediator between God and men, the *Man* Christ Jesus" (1 Tim. 2:5). He invites all of us to become one with Him, to "partake of the divine nature" (2 Pet. 1:4), and to have our humanity deified in Him. This deification in Christ, called *theosis* in Greek, elevates our humanity beyond even the original pre-fallen state in the Garden of Eden.

OTHER FACETS. There are numerous other critical lessons we derive from the Cross, such as our death in Christ and with Christ, our learning to die to ourselves in obedience to God as Christ did, joy coming to all the world through the Cross,[183] the

---

[183] From the Divine Liturgy of St. John Chrysostom.

Eucharist[184] becoming possible by the Cross, and even attaining to the vision of God through the mystery of the Cross.[185] Those beautiful teachings usually hold the primary place in traditional Orthodox theology - above ransom and debt satisfaction. We do not reject the latter, but we see that a doctrine focused on debt payments cannot fully explain the unity of God's will, His love, His mercy, our adoption as sons of God (Gal. 4:6) and our partaking of the divine nature (2 Pet. 1:4).

ON NOT GOING TOO FAR

The language of sacrifice, ransom, and debt payment is found in the Bible and many Fathers of the Church. However, we Orthodox do not place primary emphasis on this imagery. While we reject anything that distorts God's character – such as God being bound by justice, desiring an instrument of wrath, or needing revenge for His honor being offended – we do not reject the language of Christ's sacrificial death being a propitiation for our sins or a ransom from death. However, we are careful not to go beyond those images. Otherwise, if the imagery is systematized, it results in distorting the truth. More can be found on what the Orthodox Church teaches about Christ's death on the Cross in Section 1.3, "The Cure for Sin and Death."

---

[184] *Eucharist* is the Greek word for the sacrament of Holy Communion in which we receive the precious Body and Blood of Christ.

[185] *St. Gregory Palamas, The Homilies*: Homily Eleven, p. 78.

APPENDIX D: A LETTER TO CHARISMATICS

———◆———

DEAR CHARISMATIC BROTHER OR SISTER:

After nearly twenty-five years in the Charismatic movement, I needed something deeper. I began looking for the true early Church, and the Holy Spirit led me to Orthodoxy. There, I found the continuation of Pentecost, but in a way that surprised me. The presence of the Holy Spirit in Orthodoxy looks different than a former Pentecostal might expect. It's alive and subtle, vibrant and quiet, life-changing but easily unnoticed.

Such a quiet liturgical environment left me bored during my first few months attending Orthodox churches. If you find yourself in the same situation, be patient. You'll need to mentally and spiritual detoxify, as I did, from the flashing lights and noise pollution that we have grown accustomed to.

Many Christian congregations in the West have experienced evolution in their style of worship, yet the Orthodox Church remains unchanged. Orthodoxy has maintained the worship style of the first generations of Christians, which included acapella singing, prayers, and communion - all in a liturgical setting. It's beautiful, but if you're like me, it will take time to grow accustomed to it.

You may wonder why the Orthodox Church insists upon a ritualistic style of worship. Perhaps you've read no historian who indicates early Christian worship was liturgical. Sadly, many Protestant authors and historians ignore practices and beliefs in the early church if they differ from the writer's own practices and beliefs. Fortunately, you can easily research early Christianity for yourself in the writings of saints such as Ignatius of Antioch, Polycarp of Smyrna, and Clement of Rome. All three of those men knew the Apostles and preserved their teachings firsthand. They also left us letters that have been translated into English that are freely available on the internet. Another ancient witness, Justin Martyr, wrote the *First Apology,* which outlines Christian beliefs and worship in the 150s AD. He lived a mere generation after St. John wrote his Gospel and Revelation.

Unlike the numerous groups who claim to be continuing the practices of the early Church, the Orthodox Church has this paper trail proving their "heredity." When I first learned about that, I researched the above-mentioned authors and found the claims of Orthodoxy to be true: they maintain both the beliefs and worship of the early Church. But that didn't satisfy me. After all, what's the use of correct outward forms if there is no Holy Spirit breathing life within? It would make Orthodoxy little more than a religious museum filled with dry, lifeless bones.

Shortly after I reached that conclusion, someone introduced me to two works that changed my life: the *Sayings of the Desert Fathers* and a little book called *The Way of the Pilgrim*. The former revealed countless men and women who lived as radically as our Lord Jesus. They refused to mix worldliness into their devotion to God. It inspired me to struggle like them. The second book, *The Way of the Pilgrim,* took me on a journey with a 19th century Russian peasant practicing the Jesus Prayer. For an hour or two a day, I practiced quiet prayer, focusing on nothing except my Lord Jesus Christ. It was difficult at first, but slowly, my heart and mind began to be detoxified of worldly sin and noise.

The grace of the Holy Spirit moved in ways far more powerful than anything I've ever experienced in my life. After a few months, my wife said, "You're not the same person I married. And I mean that in a good way." I was no longer restless, emotionally turbulent, nor a people-pleasing coward. Immersing myself completely in Orthodox worship and prayer was changing me.

As I focused almost exclusively upon prayer, I came across the saying of a Desert Father named Abba Sisoes. A fellow desert monk asked Sisoes how he might attain to unceasing remembrance of God.[186]

---

[186] In spiritual practice today, we call this unceasing remembrance of God "prayer of the heart," which is

The abba's response shocked me. He told the young monk that such a goal is ok, but there is something better: thinking more highly of everyone else than yourself. In other words, as powerful as prayer is, humility is even more life-changing. That elder's saying began my arduous journey of learning how deeply pride is rooted in the heart.[187]

I tell you all these things, my Charismatic friend, because I know you seek a Christianity that's real, authentic, and life-giving. You've tried building your home upon the shifting sands of emotional hype, which were falsely identified as the Holy Spirit. Now you're exploring the Christian landscape, looking for solid ground. It is here in the Eastern Orthodox Church, but you'll need to find that out for yourself. Explore the books and authors that I referenced above while also getting plugged into a local Orthodox Church.[188] Orthodoxy is a lifestyle; one filled with prayer, struggle, victory, defeat, death, and rebirth. May God bless you in your journey to draw closer to Him.

---

developed through the Jesus Prayer and other hesychastic practices.

[187] See Sections 2.5 and 2.6 for more on prayer and humility.

[188] Visit orthodoxyinamerica.org to find a local community.

APPENDIX E: WILL ALL BE SAVED?

———◆———

The question of universalism is a passionately debated topic today, which is nothing new. Scholars have been asking that question regularly for at least two centuries. In Orthodoxy, some contemporary authors claim that several saints and highly esteemed theologians wrote in support of universal salvation. Since this question occasionally arises in catechism and Orthodox discussions, I have included some of my research in this booklet. Due to spatial constraints (this is an appendix, not an entire book), I have limited the scope of references to biblical books, extrabiblical writings of the Old and New Testament eras, and early Church Fathers.

The Church is the continuation of the Old Testament Israel, the people of God. That means we inherited the Jewish (Old Testament) Scriptures and much of their theology. Both those things find their fullness in Christ. By starting in the Old Testament and moving forward from there, I was able to discover a theological continuum that runs from the pre-Christian era to today.

The Orthodox Church also believes in *Apostolic Tradition*, which is sometimes referred to as the *Apostolic Deposit*. It is "the faith which was once delivered unto the saints" (Jude 3) and preserved throughout the generations up until the present day. While explanations of the faith have developed, and continue to do so, the core of the faith remains unchanged. It stays unchanged because the core Truth is Christ Himself (Jn. 14:6) Who never changes (Heb. 13:8). Since the beginning, the Holy Spirit has worked through God-fearing men and women to preserve the Christian faith. No matter how fierce the persecution or clever the heresies, we have our Lord's promise, "When He, the Spirit of truth, is come, he will guide you into all truth" (Jn. 16:13).

Therefore, we Orthodox believe that despite the numerous heresies that have influenced Christians throughout the ages, there have always been those who held fast to the truth. Because the truth always prevailed, we do not feel a need to perpetually reform (*semper reformanda*). While we continuously read the Scriptures and Church Fathers for correct doctrine (1 Tim. 4:13-16) and personal transformation (Eph. 4:23), we are looking for nothing new. Theological novelty is scandalous in Orthodoxy. It reveals a delusional presumption, a devilish pride, that the truth was hidden for ages until someone was clever enough to find it. In the passage from Jude quoted above, we are told the truth has already been delivered (1:3).

My research here is presented in chronological order. It begins with the Old Testament before moving into the "inter-testament" period - that era between the Old and New Testaments sometimes called Second Temple Judaism. Then, we turn to three teachings of our Lord Jesus Christ, which are followed by ancient Church Fathers before the First Council of Nicaea in 325 A.D. (a.k.a. Ante-Nicene Fathers). Lastly, a few later Fathers are presented to show consistency in Christian teaching throughout the ages. Most of the texts referenced herein fall roughly between the third century B.C. and the third century A.D. (from the Prophet Daniel until Origen of Alexandria).

I embarked on this study with an open mind. For years, I favored universalism because the thought of an eternal hell troubles me deeply. Alas, I did not receive the inclusive, comforting answer I hoped to find. The Scriptures, when read alongside extrabiblical sources, provide only one way to properly understand the two possible fates for all humanity.

Part 1 - Biblical Passages

Going in chronological order, we will first examine the Prophet Daniel and then end with the words of our Lord.

THE OLD TESTAMENT PERIOD

The Prophet Daniel (Sixth Century B.C.)

Beginning in the Old Testament, the resurrection is first explicitly mentioned by the Prophet Daniel, who wrote about a great tribulation followed by the resurrection, "Then many of those who sleep in the dust of the earth shall awake, some to everlasting life, and some to disgrace and everlasting shame" (Daniel 12:2). Here we see some will be resurrected to *everlasting life* and others to *disgrace and everlasting shame*. There is no mention of those in the latter category being saved nor even a hint that these states will endure for a while but then come to an end.

The word in the Greek Septuagint (LXX) translated "everlasting" here is *aiónion*. In the Hebrew, it is *olam*. In the case of the Greek, that word is usually translated to mean an infinite amount of time. The same is true with *olam*. It is often used to describe God's unbreakable promises, to express Him as the eternal one, or to represent an era which will not end.

Several verses later in the Daniel passage, a universalist may point out that Daniel mentions, "Many shall choose to be made white and refined through fire; but the lawless shall act lawlessly" (12:10). Such words about cleansing through fire do not refer to purgatorial hellfire but are in reference to the great tribulation of the antichrist. Persecution and difficult trials are sometimes referred to as "fire" in the scripture (WSir. 2:5, 1 Pet. 1:6-7, Rev. 15:2). Within Daniel's book of prophecy, we see the example of the Three Holy Youths who chose to be thrown into the fiery furnace rather than betray their faith (Dan. 3). So, the context of the book does not allow refining fire to be understood in a purgatorial way. Additionally, the text says, *Many shall choose*, yet nobody chooses hellfire or purgatorial flames. Yet the martyrs freely chose suffering for their Lord over apostasy, and by their sufferings were *made white and refined through fire.*

The Warrior Judith (2nd-7th century B.C.)[189]

The inspiring story of Judith takes place in the 12th century B.C., though it was likely written sometime between the second and seventh centuries. Judith was a beautiful Jewish widow who, through intrigue, entered the tent of Nebuchadnezzar's general who was oppressing the Hebrew people. When he was drunk, she beheaded him and saved the Israelites. At the end of her book, she sings to "the Lord who makes wars cease," saying,

> Woe to the nations that rise up against my people; the Lord Almighty will punish them on the day of judgment. He will give them over to fire and worms in their flesh; in pain they shall weep forever (Jdt. 16:2,17).

Here we see almost identical language to what our Lord used in Mark to describe hell (Gehenna), "Where their worm does not die, and the fire is not quenched" (9:44). By the time Judith was written, the eschatological expectation was that God will dispense perpetual, fiery punishment "on the day of judgment."

---

[189] The story takes place around the 7th century BC but may have survived as oral tradition until it was written down in the 2nd century BC.

The Book of Enoch (2nd Century B.C.)

This pseudepigraphal work is a composite of four or five pieces of apocalyptic literature in the Hebrew tradition, each probably written by a different author. It was completed about 150 B.C. While it is not part of the Christian scriptural canon, studying it helps us to trace the development of Jewish belief over the centuries leading up to Christ.[190]

Enoch is quoted generously in the New Testament Epistle of Jude and was treated as Scripture by a few early Christian writers including Clement of Alexandria, Origen, Tertullian, and St. Augustine.[191] As with other works written in the centuries before Christ, it speaks of a coming judgment of the world at which the righteous shall rise to be with God and the unrighteous will experience endless destruction. In the first section regarding the unrighteous, it states,

> Therefore you shall curse your days, and the years of your life shall perish, and the years of your destruction shall be multiplied and in an eternal curse you shall find no mercy (5:5).

Two verses later,

> "And all the elect shall rejoice, and there shall be forgiveness of sin, and mercy and peace and

---

[190] The Ethiopian Orthodox Church is an exception. It includes Enoch in its scriptural canon.
[191] Reid, *Jewish Apocalypses: The Book of Henoch*, 602.

> forbearance and joy...And for all of you sinners there shall be no salvation, but on you all shall abide a curse (5:7).

The author of the second section, likewise, sees no chance of redemption for those who die in sin,

> And [the Elect One] shall choose the righteous and holy from among them. For the day has drawn near that they should be saved...The sinner shall be destroyed in front of the face of the Lord of spirits, and they shall be banished from off the face of His earth, and they shall perish forever and ever (51:1-2, 53:2).

Such language is echoed in St. Paul,

> These shall be punished with everlasting destruction from the presence of the Lord and from the glory of His power (2 Thess. 1:9).

The Apocalypse of Ezra (100 B.C.-100 A.D.)[192]

Like the book of Enoch, the Apocalypse of Ezra was widely used in the early Church. It also shaped theological language for many Church services that developed in the West. One of the last Church Fathers to frequently engage it and treat it as an authoritative

---

[192] Other titles used for this work include Second or Fourth Esdras and Fourth Ezra. The date of the work has been a topic of scholarly debate. The work we currently possess was possibly written by Jews before Christ but then revised and expanded by the first generation or two of Christians. Either way, it gives important insights regarding the theology and eschatology of the first Christians.

text was St. Ambrose of Milan.[193] Like Enoch, I have included it here due to its significance in the first centuries of the Church. The book follows the same schema as most books in the apocalyptic genre - a series of visions followed by interpretations. Ezra is quite relatable for many of us because he argues with God about the perceived injustice of an eternal hell.

In the seventh chapter, the angel of the Lord reveals the "pit of torment" and the "furnace of hell" that awaits sinners, and contrasts that with the rest and delight of paradise (7:36). Seeing that nearly all men have evil dwelling in their hearts because of the Fall (3:26), Ezra is thrown into despondency. With hell being eternal, he feels that it would have been better for God to never have made man than for man to suffer forever. He cries out,

> And now I see that the world to come will bring delight to few, but torments to many. For an evil heart has grown up in us, which has alienated us from God, and has brought us into corruption and the ways of death, and has shown us the paths of perdition and removed us far from life – and that not just a few of us but almost all who have been created (7:47-48).

Ezra's despondency is understandable. He lived in a time before the mystery of our redemption in Christ had been fully revealed. Seeing the absolute holiness of the Lord and paradise, contrasted with the abysmal condition of mankind (Jews and Gentiles

---

[193] Reid, *Jewish Apocalypses: The Book of Ezra*, 603.

alike), he had no hope for himself and hardly anyone else. The Lord's answer provides him little consolation,

> I will rejoice over the few who shall be saved...For this reason, therefore, those who dwell on earth shall be tormented, because though they had understanding they committed iniquity, and though they received the commandments they did not keep them (7:60, 72).

Such a statement anticipates St. Paul in Romans,

> For since the creation of the world His invisible attributes are clearly seen, being understood by the things that are made, even His eternal power and Godhead, so that they are without excuse (Rom. 1:20).

Additionally, it is revealed to Ezra that those who have died cannot repent and therefore cannot change their state of damnation, "The second way [they are tormented]: because they cannot now make a good repentance that they may live" (7:82). While the Lord encourages Ezra in prayers for the departed during our present age, he advises that they will do nothing after the judgement at the End.[194] At that point, everyone's fate is eternally sealed (7:105-115).

Again in chapter eight, Ezra returns to how unfair it is that few will be saved yet nobody chooses

---

[194] See also 2 Maccabees 12:38-45 for another account from the Old Testament era regarding prayers for the departed.

to be born. The Lord replies with the following parable:

> The farmer sows many seeds upon the ground and plants a multitude of seedlings, and yet not all that have been sown will come up in due season, and not all that were planted will take root; so also those who have been sown in the world will not all be saved" (8:41).

When Ezra again begins to argue, the Lord rebukes him,

> You come far short of being able to love my creation more than I love it...Therefore do not ask any more questions about the multitude of those who perish. For they also received freedom, but they despised the Most High, and were contemptuous of his law, and forsook his ways (8:47, 55, 56).

Several other ancient works could be referenced which support the pre-Christian Jewish belief of everlasting reward for God's people and eternal punishment for sinners. But the above will suffice in demonstrating the consistency of belief in the theology of Second Temple Judaism. That period was also the era of the Apostles and our Lord, who continued and built upon the theological tradition of that time.

THE GOSPELS

Our Lord Jesus talked more about hellfire than any other biblical author. Since He is God, His words certainly demand the greatest respect and most careful interpretation. Due to the numerous references in our Lord's words to the Last Judgment, only those in the 25th chapter of Matthew will be examined. Other New Testament authors develop themes found in the Gospels and in the writings examined above, but overall, they add very little that is new.[195] They primarily continued the theological tradition already in place among the Jews.

The Ten Virgins

This chapter begins with the Parable of the Ten Virgins, five who took oil for their lamps, and another five who did not. When the bridegroom comes (a symbol for the Second Coming of Christ), the five foolish virgins are locked out of the kingdom. When they wish for the door to be opened to them, the Lord tells them, "Assuredly I say to you, I do not know you" (25:12). Our Lord ends the parable saying, "Watch therefore, for you know neither the day nor the hour in which the Son of Man is coming" (25:13). Such a parable offers no hope that all will be saved. Early Christian commentary on this passage will be presented in the brief review of the *Apocalypse of Peter* below.

---

[195] There is much written about the coming Wrath and Judgment in the epistles of the Apostles. But these themes are found in the Gospels and Old Testament period writings. Taking into consideration both biblical and extrabiblical works, even Revelation doesn't add new concepts regarding the final judgment of the world.

The Parable of the Talents

Next is the Parable of the Talents (25:14-30) in which three servants receive talents numbering five, two, and one. The men who received the five and the two invest wisely. However, the servant who receives the one buries it in the ground. When the master returns, he rewards the two servants who doubled their talents while punishing the one who did not. Our Lord ends the parable stating, "Cast the unprofitable servant into the outer darkness. There will be weeping and gnashing of teeth" (25:30). Again, no hope is offered that the man's punishment is a temporary one. Given the theological context of those times as presented above, there is no reason to believe that an end to the man's punishment was understood by the audience. Quite the opposite.

The Sheep and Goats

The last in this sequence of three regards the teaching of the Sheep and Goats, which is a straightforward warning of things to come. We are told by our Lord,

> When the Son of Man comes in his glory, and all the angels with him, then he will sit on his glorious throne. All the nations will be gathered before him, and he will separate them one from another (25:31-32).

These verses echo the Prophet Daniel (Dan. 12:2). At the Second Coming, all people will be resurrected from everywhere for judgment. The righteous and unrighteous will be separated from one another. To the righteous sheep, Jesus will say, "Come, you who are blessed by my Father; inherit the kingdom prepared for you from the foundation of the world" (25:34). But to unrighteous goats on the left, he will say,

> Depart from me, you who are cursed, into the eternal fire prepared for the devil and his angels...and they will go away into eternal punishment, but the righteous into eternal life (25:41, 46).

The same Greek word *aiōnion* is used to express the *eternal* reward and *eternal* punishment in this verse. Consequently, heaven and hell are both *aiōnion*, that is, *eternal*. To interpret one as temporary and the other as eternal is inconsistent at best and deceptive at worst. St. Irenaeus' early commentary on this passage is discussed below.

SAVED THROUGH FIRE
> If any man's work shall be burned, he shall suffer loss: but he himself shall be saved; yet so as by fire. (1 Cor. 3:15, KJV).

To keep things concise, I am not addressing every biblical passage on the last judgment and hellfire. However, this passage is often quoted by universalists, so it seems worthwhile to address. St. Paul seems to indicate that a purgatorial hellfire will cleanse us so that we can be saved. Early Church Fathers, such as St. Cyprian of Carthage and the author of the Shepherd of Hermas, saw in this passage confirmation that our salvation will come through the fire of persecution and worldly hardships we endure for Christ.[196] The persecuted Church read this passage radically different than we do today.

St. Ambrose of Milan comments that this passage is teaching about the fire of the Holy Spirit being received within the sacraments for our spiritual purification, for the burning up of our old, sinful works.[197] On the other hand, the ancient Roman presbyter, Ambrosiaster, sees in the passage a torment reserved for teachers of the faith who unintentionally taught incorrectly. Of such a teacher he says, "Unlike complete unbelievers, he will not be tortured in eternal fire, and so to some extent it will be worth his while to have believed in Christ."[198] Saints Gregory the Great and Caesarius of Arles, in their commentaries on this passage, also write of a post-death purging of sins. They state this is only for small sins that a repentant but imperfect Christian had not yet overcome.[199] Purging is not for unbelievers, so they taught.

St. John Chrysostom takes the hardest line of all, stating that being "saved" in St. Paul's passage means that the man is not utterly destroyed from existence. His sinful works are burned up, but his existence is

---

[196] Cyprian of Carthage, *Epistle 51 to Antonianus*. *The Shepherd of Hermas*, Third Vision, Chap. 7.

[197] Ambrose of Milan, *Duties of the Clergy,* 3.18.

[198] Ambrosiaster, *Commentary on First Corinthians*, 3.15.

[199] See ACCS Vol. VII, *1-2 Corinthians* for these and more patristic commentary on this passage.

saved. However, he will suffer hellfire for all eternity.[200] The Church Fathers offer many opinions about this difficult passage, but none of them see in it an ultimate reconciliation of all people. Such a viewpoint has been read into the passage only in modern times.

God Does Not Desire Our Punishment

All these biblical teachings provide us with a terrifying warning: there will come a time when everything we have done with our life is judged by God. Therefore, we must stay attentive and live righteously. We are warned of the consequences of spiritual sloth and disobedience. Such behavior makes us strangers to God (25:12), casts us into darkness (25:30), and sends us eternally into a fiery punishment (25:46). God does not desire to punish anyone, in fact, He desires that all be saved (1 Tim. 2:4). These warnings are for our benefit. As Theodoret of Cyrus wrote,

> After all, if he [God] wanted to punish, he would not threaten punishment; instead, by threatening he makes clear that he longs to save and not to punish.[201]

God desires our salvation, not our damnation, therefore these warnings are given to us that we might seek the way to eternal life.

Many other warnings of eternal condemnation can be found in the Gospels and the remainder of the

---

[200] John Chrysostom, *Homilies on First Corinthians*, 9.4-6.
[201] Theodoret of Cyrus, *Commentary on Hosea*.

New Testament.[202] But to avoid belaboring the point, we will turn to the early Church - including some who were closely linked to the Apostles. We will again witness the unbroken theological chain stretching from the pre-Christian era, to the time of the Lord and His Apostles, to the first several generations of Christians.

Part 2 - The Church Fathers

Countless ancient Christians wrote about the Last Judgment, and many of their works are available in English. The idea that hell was temporary – or that there would be an ultimate reconciliation of all men – first appears in the author Origen who lived in the third century. [203] A study of pre-Origen Christian texts reveals an eschatology consistent with the Old and New Testament as well as the above-mentioned extrabiblical Jewish texts. The purpose of quoting the following early Church Fathers is to show that Origen was inventing something new and alien to the Christian faith in his theology of the restoration of all things (*apocatastasis*). All emphasized text added to the quotes below is my own.

EPISTLE OF BARNABAS (c. 70-132): This epistle is traditionally attributed to St. Paul's companion Barnabas. While the authorship is widely disputed,

---

[202] E.g. Matt. 24:18, Mk. 16:15-16, Jn. 3:18

[203] Clement of Alexandria, Origen's predecessor, has also been claimed by some Universalists, but I find their evidence to be strained at best. Regardless, Origen was the first to teach about these things explicitly.

its early date is not. In it, the author writes: "But the way of darkness is crooked, and full of cursing; for it is the way of eternal death with punishment." [204]

ST. IGNATIUS OF ANTIOCH (†110): Ignatius was a disciple of the Apostle John and a friend of the martyr St. Polycarp. Writing about two heretics during his time, he warns his flock,

> Avoid also the children of the evil one, Theodotus and Cleobulus, who produce death-bearing fruit, whereof if anyone tastes, he instantly dies, and that *not a mere temporary death, but one that shall endure forever.*[205]

And in another place,

> Do not err, my brethren. Those that corrupt families shall not inherit the kingdom of God. And if those that corrupt mere human families are condemned to death, how much more shall those suffer *everlasting punishment* who endeavor to corrupt the Church of Christ! [206]

APOCALYPSE OF PETER (130-150): While this is considered a spurious work, its early date is virtually undisputed. It has not been preserved whole, but we have fragments of it when it was quoted in other works. One such quotation comes from an ancient Latin homily on the Ten Virgins in Matthew chapter 25. The homilist quotes the

---

[204] *Epistle of Barnabas*, 20.
[205] Ignatius of Antioch, *Epistle to the Trallians*, 11.
[206] Ignatius of Antioch, *Epistle to the Ephesians*, 16.

Apocalypse of Peter saying, "The closed door is the river of fire by which *the ungodly shall be kept out of the kingdom of God*, as is written in Daniel and in Peter, in his Apocalypse." [207]

ST. JUSTIN MARTYR (†165): Justin, a former philosopher turned Christian, was one of the first apologists of the Christian faith. He wrote,

> The serpent that sinned from the beginning, and the angels like him, may be destroyed, and that death may be despised, and forever quit, at the second coming of the Christ...when *some are sent to be punished unceasingly into judgment and condemnation of fire*; but others shall exist in freedom from suffering, from corruption, and from grief, and in immortality. [208]

ST. IRENAEUS OF LYONS (†202): Irenaeus was a disciple of St. Polycarp, who in turn was a disciple of the Apostle John. Therefore, he is among the earliest writers in the history of the Church. Through him, we catch glimpses of early Christian belief. Numerous quotes could be pulled from his work *Against Heresies*, however, the most relevant one emphasizes that the Greek word *aiōnion* describes a time that is not temporary. This passage was written as commentary on the Sheep and Goats in Matthew 25:31-46,

---

[207] *The Apocryphal New Testament*, electronic edition, http://earlychristianwritings.com/text/apocalypsepeter-mrjames.html, accessed 3/20/2020.
[208] Justin Martyr, *Dialogue with Trypho*, 45.

Thus also the punishment of those who do not believe the Word of God, and despise His advent, and are turned away backwards, is increased; *being not merely temporal, but rendered also eternal.* For to whomsoever the Lord shall say, 'Depart from me, ye cursed, into everlasting fire,' these *shall be damned forever*; and to whomsoever He shall say, 'Come, ye blessed of my Father, inherit the kingdom prepared for you for eternity,' these do *receive the kingdom forever*, and make constant advance in it. [209]

Here we have an ancient Greek Christian writing about the meaning of an ancient Greek word that is hotly debated in some theological circles today. The witness of an ancient Greek Christian is the most compelling since he lived near the time the New Testament was penned. St. Irenaeus would have understood, not only the Apostolic Tradition (of which he was an immediate recipient), but also the nuances of the word *aiōnion* better than any contemporary scholar. Here he explicitly writes that the word designates, not a temporary, but an eternal state.

OTHER CHURCH FATHERS

Countless Church Fathers taught against universalism. Without a doubt, the consensus is easy to see. Finding patristic consensus is important because a careful study of the Fathers will reveal speculations and theological opinions of certain

---

[209] Irenaeus, *Against Heresies*, Book IV, 28.2.

Fathers that were not held by a majority of the Fathers. Because we believe in the words of our Lord who said that the Holy Spirit would come and teach His Church "all things" (John 14:26) and will "guide you into all truth" (John 16:13), we do not believe it is possible for nearly all holy men everywhere in the Church to err on such an important matter of doctrine.

ORIGEN (†254): His Legacy and His Errors

Origen left a lasting literary legacy that influenced the writings of many Church Fathers. However, he was a brilliant man who enjoyed theological speculations. Due to the popularity of his work, later councils and Fathers would have to condemn the man whom they deeply loved and respected, who died after many torments as a confessor of the Church. [210]

A set of fifteen anathemas were finally leveled against many of Origen's teachings. These anathemas - associated with the Fifth Ecumenical Council - have been accepted by the Church since that time. Many of them will seem strange to the modern reader not well-versed in Platonism, which heavily influenced Origen. The condemnations regard his teachings on the origin and fall of the visible and invisible creation (his cosmology) and what he taught about the resurrected body and the last things (his eschatology). In other words, the Church condemned his speculations about the first and last things.

---

[210] Danielou, *Origen*, 26.

Origen's cosmology, like Christian theology, taught that before the physical world was created, the spiritual world existed. Unlike Christian theology though, he speculated that the spirits of all rational beings - called *logika* in Greek - were in a heavenly realm contemplating the one God, whom we call God the Father. Eventually, the spirits became satiated with their contemplation of God and they "fell." Those who fell to a lesser degree became angels, those who fell the most became demons. In between these two extremes were the *logika* that would become the souls of humans. God created the physical cosmos to stop our *logika* from further fall. This physical world offers us a place to work out our salvation through the difficulties of life. [211]

Origen's eschatology teaches that eventually all of creation will be renewed in the *apocatastasis*, which is Greek for restitution or restoration. It is the belief that all souls will be restored to their former condition of contemplating God - whether it is the soul of a human, an angel, or a demon.[212] Origen could find no theological use for our physical bodies after the Last Judgment since "he cannot conceive of a continuing role for corporeality once all things have returned to their union with God." [213] The dissolution of the body would bring things full circle, "'For the

---

[211] Cf. Origen's *Commentary on Matthew* Book 14.9.

[212] The word "soul" here is being used in a general way to mean the non-physical aspect of our humanity.

[213] Trigg, *Origen*, 31.

end,' as Origen repeatedly stated, 'is always like the beginning.'" [214]

The Fifth Ecumenical Council condemned these errors in its fifteen anathemas against Origenism. The first anathema proclaimed, "If anyone asserts the fabulous pre-existence of souls, and shall assert the monstrous restoration which follows from it: let him be anathema." The last one affirms,

> If anyone shall say that the life of the spirits shall be like to the life which was in the beginning while as yet the spirits had not come down or fallen, so that the end and the beginning shall be alike, and that the end shall be the true measure of the beginning: let him be anathema. [215]

As can be seen from quotes throughout this chapter from the Old Testament, New Testament, and the pre-Origen Church Fathers, Origen's "eschatology ran counter to two fundamental early Christian beliefs: the belief that God will condemn the wicked to eternal punishment and the belief that the final Christian hope is for the faithful to be restored to their bodies in the resurrection of the dead." [216]

ST. JOHN OF DAMASCUS (†749)

Skipping ahead several centuries, we come to the Damascene. This monk completed a lofty work in the

---

[214] Louth, *Maximus the Confessor*, 66. See pages 26-32 in Trigg and Louth's *Maximus the Confessor*, 65-68, for more details on Origen's cosmology and eschatology.
[215] *Nicene Post-Nicene Fathers,* Series Two, Volume 14.
[216] Trigg, 30.

eighth century often entitled *An Exact Exposition on the Orthodox Faith*. It summarizes the theology of the Church Fathers up to his time and can act as a quick reference to investigate the dogma of the Church on any number of matters. Regarding demons, he writes,

> The unquenchable fire and everlasting torment have been prepared for the Devil and his evil spirits and for them who follow him. One should note that the fall is to the angels just what death is to men. For, just as there is no repentance for men after their death, so is there none for the angels after their fall. [217]

The reason there is no repentance for demons is not because God does not desire it. Rather, they are not composite creatures like us. We have physical bodies with needs and desires that compete with our spiritual aspect, causing us to vacillate. Angels and demons are non-composite beings. In their simplicity, they have a singular will to either serve God or rebel against Him. Once they have made their choice, they do not waffle or second-guess themselves like humans. Additionally, they live in what might be called *angelic time* which is different from the *temporal time* that we live in. We constantly experience sequential moments in our *temporal time* where we choose either to turn a little more towards God or towards our own selfish will. But due to the nature of the demons and their mode of time, there is

---

[217] John Damascene, *An Exact Exposition*, 2.4.

no repentance because they have eternally made up their minds.

Regarding the lack of repentance for men after death, two things can be said. First, this means that a man is who he is when he dies. There is no changing that. His heart was either oriented toward God and repentance, at least to some small degree, or it was hardened against God and consistently sought its own will over God's will. Second, that does not mean that praying for the departed - as taught in the Orthodox Church - is a useless practice. For those who had at least some inclination toward God, and who were living according to His commands the best they knew how (even if that left much to be desired), then we pray that God would forgive their shortcomings and receive them into His kingdom. They are still incapable of repenting. But whatever little fruits of repentance they had in their life, we are asking God to magnify those things. If there never was any repentance, then there is nothing to work with. See the *Apocalypse of Ezra* (as noted above) and 2 Maccabees 12:38-45 for pre-Christian witnesses regarding prayers for the departed.

St. John of Damascus concludes his book by explaining the Final Judgment:

> And so, with our souls again united to our bodies, which will have become incorrupt and put off corruption, we shall rise again and stand before the terrible judgment seat of Christ. And the Devil and his demons, and his man (the Antichrist), and the impious and sinners will be given over to everlasting fire, which will not be a material fire

such as we are accustomed to, but a fire such as God might know. And those who have done good will shine like the sun together with the angels unto eternal life with our Lord Jesus Christ, ever seeing Him and being seen, enjoying the unending bliss which is from Him, and praising Him together with the Father and the Holy Ghost unto the endless ages of ages. Amen. [218]

ST. GREGORY PALAMAS (†1359)

One of the greatest theologians of the second millennium was St. Gregory Palamas, who famously defended the hesychastic tradition. In his homilies he affirms the Orthodox teaching of the eternality of both heaven and hell. While commenting on the Parable of the Rich Man and Lazarus, he discusses the gulf or abyss separating Lazarus from the rich man in the afterlife, "These words of his are proof that the damnation of sinners is unending and unchanging, as is the comfort of the righteous." [219] But he provides comfort to those who are struggling. He discusses the restoration of those in the kingdom, which is our transformation into being "a son and heir of God, a joint-heir with Christ." Such a person:

> In the age to come will, with all certainty, receive the divine and immortal adoption as a son, which will not be taken from him, unless he has forfeited this by spiritual death. Sin is spiritual death, and whereas physical death is annulled when the future age arrives, spiritual death is confirmed for

[218] John Damascene, *An Exact Exposition*, 4.27.
[219] Palamas, Homily 48.12.

those who bring it with them from here...but someone born of Christ, even though he fall into deadly sins, if he turns again and runs to the Father who raises the dead, is made alive once more, obtains divine adoption, and is not cast out from the company of the just. [220]

ST. PAISIOS OF MT. ATHOS (†1994)

The final word of this section will be given to a much-beloved saint of our modern era, Paisios of Mt. Athos, who once said,

Let us struggle with all our powers to gain Paradise. The gate is very narrow. Don't listen to those who say that everyone will be saved. This is a trap of Satan so that we won't struggle. [221]

Part 3 - Final Thoughts

It has always been important to me that my Christian faith is in accordance with what the early Church taught. Christianity is not a philosophical system about God but the path to know Him. There is a stream of life that flows from the time of Christ to the present day. Within the stream are the sacred Scriptures, the inspired writings of the Fathers, and the practices of the early Church. This stream is life in the Holy Spirit, which is also called the Tradition of the Church. When we cut ourselves off from the stream because we feel we are more clever or wiser,

---

[220] Palamas, Homily 57.16,18.
[221] *Precious Vessels of the Holy Spirit*, 138

then we cut ourselves off from Christ and life in the Holy Spirit.

If we are unable to find a theological idea in the accepted Church Tradition, we must admit that it is new. While expressing ancient truths in creative, new ways is encouraged, inventing innovative doctrine is not. Being creative - in the bad sense - is losing continuity with the early Church and, thereby, inventing a new religion.

With a doctrine as significant as the salvation of all humanity, we must begin our investigation at the beginning. Those who choose Origen as their starting point, and reinterpret biblical passages through the lens of Origen, are severing themselves from the life of the earlier Church. They are also ignoring the rich theological and literary context in which the Christian Scriptures were written and interpreted by the earliest Christians. It is not possible that our Lord Jesus and all the prophets and apostles were wrong on this topic until Origen.

Our discomfort with the concept of eternal punishment is nothing new. But we must trust God that He loves humanity far more than we ever could, as the Lord told Ezra in the above quoted text. God will find a way to save everyone who is willing to be saved. The Christian Church, from her earliest days, inherited the eschatology of her Jewish roots, while simultaneously explaining it more deeply through the revelation of Jesus Christ. That revelation must be preserved throughout the ages, even if it makes us uncomfortable.

BIBLIOGRAPHY

Ancient Christian Commentary on Scripture, Vol. VII, 1-2 Corinthians. Edited by Thomas C. Oden and Gerald Bray. New York and Longdon: Routledge Publishers, 1999.

Ambrosiaster: Commentaries on Romans and 1-2 Corinthians. Edited by Thomas C. Oden and Gerald Bray. Downers Grove, IL: InterVarsity Press, 2009.

Andersson, Hilary. "Social Media Apps Are Deliberately Addictive to Users," *British Broadcasting Company*, 4 July 2018. Accessed 20 March 2021, https://www.bbc.com/news/technology-44640959.

Athanasius. *On the Incarnation.* Translated by John Behr. Yonkers, NY: St. Vladimir's Seminary Press, 2011.

Augustine of Hippo. "On the Trinity." *Nicene Post-Nicene Fathers, Series 1, Vol. 4.* Edited by Philip Schaff and Henry Wace. Peabody, MA: Hendricks Publishers, 2012.

Basil the Great of Caesarea. *Against Eunomius.* Trans. by Mark Delcogliano and Andrew Radde-Gallwitz. Washington, DC: The Catholic University of America Press, 2011.

Boosalis, Harry. *Person to Person: The Orthodox Understanding of Human Nature*. South Canaan, PA: St. Tikhon's Monastery Press, 2018.

Brooks, Mike. "How Much Screen Time Is Too Much?" *Psychology Today*, 26 December 2018. Accessed 18 March, 2021, https://www.psychologytoday.com/us/blog/tech-happy-life/201812/how-much-screen-time-is-too-much

Catena Aurea: Commentary of the Church Fathers on the Gospel According to St. Matthew, Compiled by Thomas Aquinas. Translated by John Henry Newman 1874, revised by Jeremy McKemy (unpublished manuscript).

Chesterton, Gilbert K. *Heretics / Orthodoxy.* Nashville, TN: Thomas Nelson, Inc., 2000.

Early Christian Writings website was accessed for public domain editions of Apocryphal New Testament era writings. http://earlychristianwritings.com/

Ephraim the Syrian. *Hymns on Paradise.* Translated by Sebastian Brock. Crestwood, NY: St. Vladimir's Seminary Press, 1990.

Gregory of Nazianzus. "Epistle 101: To Cledonius the Priest Against Apollinarius." *Nicene Post-Nicene Fathers, Series 2, Vol. 7*. Edited by Philip Schaff and Henry Wace. Peabody, MA: Hendricks Publishers, 2012.

_____. "Fourth Theological Oration (Oration 30)." *Nicene Post-Nicene Fathers, Series 2, Vol. 7*. Edited by Philip Schaff and Henry Wace. Peabody, MA: Hendricks Publishers, 2012.

_____. "Second Oration on Easter (Oration 45)." *Nicene Post-Nicene Fathers, Series 2, Vol. 7*. Edited by Philip Schaff and Henry Wace. Peabody, MA: Hendricks Publishers, 2012.

Gregory of Nyssa. *Catechetical Disourse*. Translated by Ignatius Green. Yonkers, NY: St. Vladimir's Seminary Press, 2019.

_____. "On Not Three Gods: To Ablabius." *Nicene Post-Nicene Fathers, Series 2, Vol. 5*. Edited by Philip Schaff and Henry Wace. Peabody, MA: Hendricks Publishers, 2012.

_____. "On the Holy Trinity, and of the Godhead of the Holy Spirit: To Eustathius." *Nicene Post-Nicene Fathers, Series 2, Vol. 5*. Edited by Philip Schaff and Henry Wace. Peabody, MA: Hendricks Publishers, 2012.

_____. "On the Holy Spirit: Against the Followers of Macedonius." *Nicene Post-Nicene Fathers, Series 2, Vol. 5*. Edited by Philip Schaff and Henry Wace. Peabody, MA: Hendricks Publishers, 2012.

Gregory Palamas. Saint Gregory Palamas: The Homilies. Translated by Christopher Veniamin. Dalton, PA: Mount Thabor Publishing, 2014.

Hapgood, Isabel Florence. Service Book of the Holy Orthodox Catholic Apostolic (Greco-Russian) Church, (Boston and New York: Houghton, Mifflin, and Co., 1906).

Hesiod. *Hesiod, the Homeric Hymns, and Homerica.* Translated by Hugh G. Evelyn-White. New York, MacMillan Co., 1914.

Hieratikon, Vol. 2: Liturgy Book for Priest & Deacon. Edited by Hieromonk Herman and Vitaly Permiakov. South Canaan, PA: St. Tikhon's Monastery Press, 2017.

Hierotheos of Nafpaktos. *Orthodox Psychotherapy.* Translated Esther Williams. Levadia, Greece, Birth of the Theotokos Monastery, 2012.

Holman Bible Publishers, *CSB Ancient Faith Study Bible.* Nashville, TN: Holman Bible Publishers, 2019.

Hurnard, Hannah. *Hinds' Feet on High Places.* Westwood, NJ: Barbour & Company, Inc., 1977.

Irenaeus of Lyon. *Against Heresies*, Ante-Nicene Fathers, Vol. 1. Edited by Alexander Roberts & James Donaldson. Peabody, MA: Hendrickson Publishers, 1994.

Isaac the Syrian, *The Ascetical Homilies, Revised Second Edition.* Translated by Holy Transfiguration Monastery. Brookline, MA: Holy Transfiguration Monastery, 2011.

James, M.R. *The Apocryphal New Testament.* Oxford: Clarendon Press, 1924.

John Chrysostom. *Homilies on Genesis 1-17.* Translated by Robert C. Hill. Washington, DC: The Catholic University of America Press, 1986.

_____. "Homilies on Corinthians." *Nicene Post-Nicene Fathers, Series 1, Vol. 12.* Edited by Philip Schaff and Henry Wace. Peabody, MA: Hendricks Publishers, 2012.

John Climacus. *The Ladder of Divine Ascent.* Translated by Archimandrite Lazarus Moore. London: Faber & Faber, 1959.

John the Damascene. *An Exact Exposition on the Orthodox Faith.* Translated by Frederic Chase. Ex Fontibus Co., 2015.

Justin Martyr. *First Apology,* Ante-Nicene Fathers, Vol. 1. Edited by Rev. Alexander Roberts and James Donaldson, Edinburgh: T&T Clark, 1867.

King University Online. "Cell Phone Addiction: The Statistics of Gadget Dependency," 27 July 2017. Accessed 12 February 2021, https://online.king.edu/news/cell-phone-addiction/.

Krivosheine, Basil. "The Ascetic and Theological Teaching of Gregory Palamas," *The Eastern Churches Quarterly*, No. 4. London: EJ Coldwell Ltd, 1938.

Larchet, Jean-Claude. *Theology of the Body*. Yonkers, NY: St. Vladimir's Seminary Press, 2016.

_____, *Theology of Illness*. Yonkers, NY: St. Vladimir's Seminary Press, 2002.

Lewis, Clive Staples. *Essay Collection & Other Short Pieces*, edited by Lesley Walmsley. London, HarperCollins Publishers, 2000.

Ligonier Ministries. "The State of Theology," 2020. Accessed 23 January 2021, https://thestateoftheology.com/.

Little Russian Philokalia: St. Seraphim of Sarov. Translated by Seraphim Rose. Platina, CA: St. Herman's Press, 2008.

Living without Hypocrisy: Spiritual Counsels of the Holy Elders of Optina. Translated by Bp. George Schaefer. Jordanville, NY: Holy Trinity Publications, 2005.

Louth, Andrew, *Maximus the Confessor*. London and New York: Routledge, 1996.

_____, *The Origins of the Christian Mystical Tradition*. Oxford: Clarendon Press, 1981.

Macarius the Great. *Pseudo-Macarius: The Fifty Spiritual Homilies and the Great Letter*. Translated by George A. Maloney. Mahwah, NJ: Paulist Press, 1992.

MacDonald, George. *Unspoken Sermons Vol. 3*, "Justice," 1889. Public Domain.

Maximus the Confessor. "Four Centuries on Love," *The Philokalia*, Vol. 2. Translated by G.E.H Palmer, Philip Sherrard, and Kallistos Ware. New York: Faber and Faber, 1981.

McDowell, Joshua. *More than a Carpenter*. Carol Stream, IL: Tyndale House Publishers, 2005.

Naha, Namrata. "Orfield Laboratories: The World's Quietest Place, Quiet Enough to Hear Your Blood Flowing," *STSTW Media*, 10 September 2018. Accessed on 2/22/2021. https://www.ststworld.com/orfield-laboratories/.

Native American Myths and Legends. Selected and edited by Richard Erdoes and Alfonso Ortiz. New York: Pantheon Books, 1984.

Origen of Alexandria. *Origen's Commentary on the Gospel of Matthew*. Ante-Nicene Fathers, Vol. XI. Edited by Allan Menzies. Peabody, MA: Hendrickson Publishers, 1896.

Orthodox Christian Prayers. Edited by Priest John Mikitish and Hieromonk Herman. South Canaan, PA: St. Tikhon's Monastery Press, 2019.

Paisios the Athonite. *Passions and Virtues*. Thessaloniki, Greece: Holy Monaastery of Evangelist John the Theologian, 2016.

_____. *Spiritual Struggle*. Thessaloniki, Greece: Holy Monaastery of Evangelist John the Theologian, 2010.

Pilgrimage of the Heart: A Treasury of Eastern Christian Spirituality, edited by George A. Maloney. San Francisco: Harper & Row, 1983.

Popovich, Justin. *Orthodox Faith and Life in Christ.* Translated by Asterios Gerostergios. Belmont, MA: Institute for Byzantine and Modern Greek Studies, 1994.

Precious Vessels of the Holy Spirit: The Live and Counsels of Contemporary Elders of Greece. Edited & translated by Andrew G. Middleton. Greenville, SC: Protecting Veil, 2011.

Pulpit Commentary, The Acts of the Apostles, Edited by Rev. Canon H.D.M. Spence and Rev. Joseph S. Exell, (New York & Toronto: Funk & Wagnells Co., 1890).

Pusey, Reverend EB, *What Is of Faith to Everlasting Punishment?* Oxford: James Parker & Co, Oxford Press, 1880.

Russell, Norman. *The Doctrine of Deification in the Greek Patristic Tradition.* New York: Oxford University Press, 2004.

Sophrony of Athos. *St. Silouan the Athonite.* Crestwood, NY: St. Vladimir's Seminary Press, 1991.

Symeon the New Theologian. *The First Created Man.* Translated by Seraphim Rose. Platina, CA: St. Herman's Press, 2013.

Symeon the New Theologian. *On the Mystical Life: The Ethical Discourses*, Vol. 1: The Church and the Last Things. Translated by Alexander Golitzen. Crestwood, NY: St. Vladimir's Seminary Press, 1995.

Reid, George J. "Jewish Apocalypses: The Book of Henoch." In *The Catholic Encyclopedia*, edited by Charles G. Herbermann, 602-603. New York: Robert Appleton Company, 1907.

_____. "Jewish Apocalypses: Fourth Book of Esdras." In *The Catholic Encyclopedia*, edited by Charles G. Herbermann, 603-604. New York: Robert Appleton Company, 1907.

Theophan the Recluse. *The Spiritual Life: And How to Be Attuned to It.* Translated by Alexandra Dockham. Safford, AZ: St. Paisius Serbian Orthodox Monastery, 2003.

Tooker, Elisabeth. *Native North American Spirituality of the Eastern Woodlands: Sacred Myths, Dreams, Visions, Speeches, Healing Formulas, Rituals, and Ceremonies.* New York: Paulist Press, 1979.

Trigg, Joseph W., *Origen*, London and New York: Routledge, 1998.

Wellness Editor. "Screen Time May Be Damaging Attention Spans," 8 June 2020. Accessed 12 February 2021, https://www.wellness.com/blog/13299742/screentime-may-be-damaging-attention-spans/wellness-editor.

Word into Spirit: Pastoral Perspectives on Confession, edited by Vasileios Thermos & Stephen Muse. South Canaan, PA: St. Tikhon's Monastery Press, 2019.

Zacharou, Zacharias. *The Enlargement of the Heart*. Edited by Christopher Veniamin. South Canaan, PA: Mount Thabor Publishing, 2006.

Printed in Great Britain
by Amazon

81017945R00122